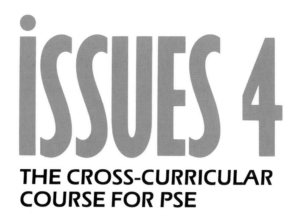

ISSUES 4

THE CROSS-CURRICULAR COURSE FOR PSE

John Foster

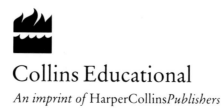

Collins Educational

An imprint of HarperCollinsPublishers

	ISSUES 1	ISSUES 2	ISSUES 3	ISSUES 4	ISSUES 5
Economic & Industrial Understanding	Understanding Industry You and Your Money Developing A Product	Consumer Affairs Understanding Businesses Gambling	Shopping Matters Trade and Development Understanding Industry: Marketing	Consumer Rights Unemployment Trade Unions	Financing Businesses Managing Your Money Rich World/Poor World
Self-Awareness/Careers	Changing Schools Homework Bullying You and Your Feelings Reviewing Your Progress	Managing Your Time Family Life Friends and Friendships You and Your Feelings Reviewing Your Progress	Living With Other People Becoming Assertive Images and Stereotypes Thinking About Your Future	Managing Your Emotions Friends and Relationships Thinking Ahead	Marriage and Partnerships Coping with Crises – Rejection and Grief You and Your Future Recording Your Achievements
Health Education	Smoking Play Safe Food and Health	Safety Matters Drugs and Drugtaking Drinking and Alcoholism	Adolescence and You Health Matters Mental Health	Health Matters The National Health Service You and Your Lifestyle	Medicine and Morality Family Planning and Parenthood Safer Sex Health and Safety at Work
Education For Citizenship	Communities and Lifestyles Rules, Rights and Responsibilities Britain's Government	People With Disabilities You and Your Rights The Nation's Finances	The Police and You Elderly People The European Community	Women's Rights Prejudice and Discrimination Crimes and Punishments	Human Rights – Refugees Housing and Homelessness A Caring Community The United Nations
Environmental Education	Waste and Recycling Planning Your Environment Air Pollution	Forests, Woods and Trees Transport and the Environment Water	Resources: Appropriate Technology The Countryside Resources: The New Technologies	Urban Environments Energy and the Environment Population and the Environment	A World Conservation Strategy Planning for the Future Pressures for Change

Published in 1993 by Collins Educational
An imprint of HarperCollins*Publishers*
77–85 Fulham Palace Road
London W6 8JB

www.**Collins**Education.com
On-line support for schools and colleges

© HarperCollins*Publishers* 1992

John Foster asserts the moral right to be identified as the author of this work.

Reprinted 1993, 1994, 1995, 1997(twice), 1998, 1999, 2000, 2002

ISBN 0 00 327337 7

Designed by Glynis Edwards
Illustrated by Nancy Anderson, Jerry Collins, Glynis Edwards, Ann Johns (Maggie Mundy Agency) and Rhian Nest James (Maggie Mundy Agency).
Typeset by Dorchester Typesetting Group Ltd
Printed and Bound by Printing Express Ltd., Hong Kong.
Series editor: Graham Bradbury
Editor: Paula Hammond

CONTENTS

UNIT 1 Women's Rights

The Sex Discrimination Acts	6
How women lag behind	7
A new deal for women?	8
Feminism and equality	9
Sexual harassment	10
Page 3 – pornography or harmless fun?	11

UNIT 2 Consumer Rights

Shopping and the law	12
A satisfactory service?	14
Mail order	15

UNIT 3 Health Matters

Pre-Menstrual Syndrome	16
Look after your skin	18
Tattoos	19

UNIT 4 Urban Environments

Third World urbanization	20
Britain's cities	22

UNIT 5 Prejudice and Discrimination

What is prejudice?	24
Racism	24
Discrimination and the law	26
Homosexuality	30
Homosexuality and the law	31

UNIT 6 Managing Your Emotions

What makes you angry?	32
Channelling your anger	33
Feeling anxious	34
Coping with stress	35

UNIT 7 Unemployment

What are the causes of unemployment?	36
What are the effects of unemployment?	38
What is it like being unemployed?	39

UNIT 8   Energy and the Environment

An energy crisis?	40
Improving efficiency, cutting pollution and conserving energy	41
Nuclear power – a risk worth taking?	42
Energy without end	44

UNIT 9   The National Health Service

The cost of the NHS	46
How do we compare?	47
Getting medical treatment	48

UNIT 10   Friends and Relationships

Choosing your friends	50
The four types of love	52
What is love?	53
What makes relationships work?	54

UNIT 11   Trade Unions

What are trade unions?	56
Why join a union?	57
The right to strike?	58
Towards a striking new image	59
Trade unions and politics	60
What do people think of trade unions?	61

UNIT 12   You and Your Lifestyle

How healthy is your lifestyle?	62
Drinking and drugs – it's your choice	64

UNIT 13   Crimes and Punishments

Why do young people commit crimes?	66
Shoplifting	67
Car crimes	68
Types of sentence	70
What's your verdict?	70

UNIT 14   Population and the Environment

A choice of futures	72
The threat to the environment	74

UNIT 15   Thinking Ahead

Choices at 16+	76
What is youth training?	78
Reviewing your progress	79

INTRODUCTION

Issues 4 is the fourth book in a series of five books, which together form a comprehensive and coherent personal and social education course for pupils of all abilities at Key Stages 3 and 4. The course is structured so that it provides schools with a framework for delivering the cross-curricular dimensions, skills and themes through a separately timetabled PSE programme. Each pupils' book, therefore, contains at least three units on each of the five cross-curricular themes – Careers Education and Guidance (including self-awareness), Health Education, Education for Citizenship, Environmental Education and Education for Economic and Industrial Understanding. For ease of reference, each unit is colour-coded according to its cross-curricular theme. The various activities within each book involve the use of all the cross-curricular skills and the choice of materials and activities has been informed by an awareness of the cross-curricular dimensions.

The fifteen units in *Issues 4* together offer a complete year's programme for Year 10. However, each unit is self-contained. The structure is, therefore, flexible enough to allow teachers to use the sections selectively within the school's own personal and social education course.

SELF-AWARENESS/CAREERS

The three Self-Awareness/Careers units concentrate on developing pupils' self-knowledge and their abilities to make decisions, manage their emotions and handle their relationships. *Friends and Relationships* considers how people choose friends and the basic rules of friendship, explores different kinds of love and examines behaviour that can make or break relationships. *Managing Your Emotions* is designed to help pupils to understand what triggers anger, how to use it constructively and to understand what stress is and how to cope with their anxieties. The final unit, *Thinking Ahead* encourages the pupils to start thinking about the options open to them at 16+ and offers an opportunity for self-assessment.

HEALTH EDUCATION

The Health Education units are designed to complement the work on health education taking place elsewhere in the curriculum. *You and Your Lifestyle* aims to promote physical health through a knowledge of fitness and diet and of the effects of alcohol and other drugs on the human body. *Health Matters* explains what Pre-Menstrual Syndrome is and how to cope with it and looks at skin care, focusing on acne and the reasons why people get tattooed. *The National Health Service* describes how Britain's health service is run, compares it with the health service in France and looks at the aims of recent reforms. It also provides information on patients' rights.

ENVIRONMENTAL EDUCATION

The three Environmental Education units are designed to fit alongside other work on environmental issues being done in National Curriculum subjects. *Energy and the Environment* explains our current dependence on fossil fuels and the environmental consequences, explores the nuclear option and looks at various renewable energy resources. *Population and the Environment* is designed to make pupils aware of the rate at which the world's population is growing, why this poses such a threat to the environment and measures that can be taken to reduce birth-rates. *Urban Environments* is divided into two sections – one focusing on the causes and effects of urbanization in Third World countries, the other looking at inner city decay and urban sprawl in Britain.

EDUCATION FOR CITIZENSHIP

The three units which form the Education for Citizenship strand of the course focus on crimes and punishments, discrimination and equal rights. *Crimes and Punishments* examines why young people commit crimes and explains the types of sentence which young offenders can be given. *Prejudice and Discrimination* is divided into two sections. The first section is designed to increase students' understanding of what racism is, of the law on racial discrimination and of what it means to be black and British. The second section focuses on homosexuality, explaining current laws and how they discriminate against homosexuals. *Women's Rights* contains information on the Sex Discrimination Act, presents facts about discrimination and explores sexual harassment and glamour modelling.

EDUCATION FOR ECONOMIC AND INDUSTRIAL UNDERSTANDING

The three Economic and Industrial Understanding units deal with trade unions, unemployment and consumer rights. *Trade Unions* provides information about trade unions, examines trade union reforms introduced by recent governments and explores the arguments put forward by both supporters and critics of trade unions. *Unemployment* describes different types of unemployment, and their causes, and examines the effects of unemployment. *Consumer Rights* focuses on shopping and the law, explaining the laws which protect the consumer.

Within each unit, the topics are presented in the form of double-page spreads, each of which provides enough material for a weekly social education session. The approach is active – learning by doing and discussing – and the activities are designed so that they can take place in an ordinary classroom.

THE SEX DISCRIMINATION ACTS

The Sex Discrimination Act, 1975 and the Equal Pay Act, 1970 became law in December 1975. Both acts have since had their scope broadened, in particular by the Sex Discrimination Act, 1986.

The Sex Discrimination Acts make it unlawful to treat anyone, on the grounds of sex, less favourably than a person of the opposite sex is, or would be, treated in the same circumstances. Sex discrimination is not allowed in employment, education, the provision of goods, facilities and services and in advertising.

What is sex discrimination?

There are two kinds of discrimination.

DIRECT discrimination involves treating a woman less favourably than a man because she is a woman (and vice versa).

INDIRECT discrimination means applying conditions equally to both sexes that cannot be shown to be justified, because they favour one sex more than the other.

For example, if an employer, in recruiting clerks, insists on candidates being 1.75 metres tall, a case could be made out that he is discriminating unlawfully against women.

Employment

Employers may not discriminate against a person because of their sex, either in their recruitment or treatment of employees. This also applies to promotion and training. Employers can no longer lawfully label jobs 'for men' or 'for women', except in certain limited circumstances. For example, in jobs where a person's sex is 'a genuine occupational qualification', as in acting; or where the job is wholly or mainly abroad where cultural differences may make it difficult for a woman applicant to carry out her job. In employment, it is also unlawful to discriminate against people because they are married. Women are entitled under the Equal Pay Act, 1970 to be paid the same as men when doing work that is the same, or broadly similar, or to equal pay for work of equal value.

Education

Co-educational schools, colleges and universities must not discriminate in the provision of facilities or in their admissions. The Careers Service must not discriminate in the advice and assistance offered to girls and boys.

Single-sex schools may, of course, restrict admissions to one sex, but this should not lead to the provision of a restricted curriculum.

Housing, goods, facilities and services

With a few exceptions, no one providing housing, goods, facilities or services to the public can lawfully discriminate against anyone because of their sex.

Discrimination must not be used against anyone who is buying or renting accommodation. A hotel, boarding house or restaurant may not refuse you accommodation or refreshments because of your sex.

A bank, building society or finance house must offer people credit, mortgages or other loans on the same terms, regardless of their sex.

VICTIMIZATION

It is unlawful to victimize a woman just because she has tried to exercise her rights under the Sex Discrimination or Equal Pay Acts.

The Equal Opportunities Commission

The Equal Opportunities Commission was created to ensure effective enforcement of the Sex Discrimination Acts and the Equal Pay Act, and to promote equal opportunities between the sexes.

As well as investigating areas of inequality between the sexes, the Commission makes recommendations to the Government about the operation of the existing laws. One of the most important functions of the Equal Opportunities Commission is to advise women of their rights under the Sex Discrimination Acts and the Equal Pay Act – and to encourage women to exercise these rights.

Who can help?

The Equal Opportunities Commission can be contacted at

Overseas House, Quay Street, Manchester M3 3HN

HOW WOMEN LAG BEHIND

Why women lose out

'Teenage girls still don't get enough encouragement to set their sights high.'

'Many women lose out on the career ladder, because they stop work to have children. By law, women ought to be entitled to career breaks and to return automatically to the same job they were doing when they became pregnant.'

'We need tougher laws. Firms and organizations should be forced to have a certain quota of women on the payroll.'

'At present, if a woman feels discriminated against, it's up to her to prove her case. It ought to be the other way round. Employers should have to prove that they don't discriminate.'

'When it comes to promotion women often get passed over. The top jobs are still reserved for men.'

'Women are brought-up to see themselves as more suited for certain jobs, such as the caring professions, where the pay isn't as good as it is in business and industry.'

'Women still take the major responsibility for child-care and there's neither enough facilities nor enough flexibility in working arrangements to make it easy for them to juggle the demands of their children and their career.'

MORE British women go out to work than in almost any other European country — and they get paid the least.

In France and Germany, female workers earn up to 10 per cent more. Only the poorer EC countries pay them as little as mean British bosses.

The shock finding, revealed in the first official comparison of women's wages, blows the lid on claims by industry and Government officials of record job opportunities for women.

Inflexible

Equal Opportunities Commission chairman Joanna Foster said: "The figures mask the fact that they are still being paid less for their work than men at home and less than many women abroad."

Women, particularly those with children, are used as cheap labour by British employers. The Commission blames the British attitude to work, which penalises men as well as women.

"The working week is longer here than in any other country in Europe," said Mrs Foster.

"It is inflexible, keeps men away from their families and puts the burden of childcare onto women, keeping them out of the job market."

The report also highlights the waste of talent in women forced to stay at home. Of the four million not working, at least a quarter have A-levels or similar qualifications.

Today (25/9/91)

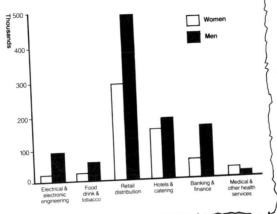

Managers in Industry

(Bar chart comparing Women and Men managers, in thousands, by industry: Electrical & electronic engineering; Food drink & tobacco; Retail distribution; Hotels & catering; Banking & finance; Medical & other health services. Vertical axis 0–500 thousands.)

Discrimination at work – the facts

- Women full-time workers earn on average only 77 per cent of the hourly earnings of comparable male workers.

- Only one-quarter of managers are women.

- Sixty out of 651 MPs are women (there are only two women in the cabinet) and of those appointed to serve on public bodies by the government, less than a fifth are women.

- Most women are ineligible for full state pensions because of career breaks from work.

Women have equal rights to enter most occupations but are concentrated in low paid jobs. Below are listed 7 well-paid occupations and 7 low-paid occupations with the percentages of women working in each.

HIGH-PAID		LOW-PAID	
Surgeons	2%	Nurses	92%
Electrical Engineers	1%	Telephone Operators	90%
Dentists	19%	Electrical Assembly	78%
Solicitors	15%	Typists/Secretaries	98%
Architects	7%	Shop Assistants	84%
Accountants	9%	Domestic Staff	98%
Financial Managers	10%	Clerks	70%

Women At Work, Equal Opportunities Commission

IN GROUPS

Why do you think women's pay still lags behind men's pay?

Why do you think there are still more men than women in high paid jobs?

Discuss each of the statements in the section 'Why women lose out'. Say whether or not you agree with the statement and why.

A NEW DEAL FOR WOMEN?

'This country now lags well behind others in Western Europe in terms of equal pay; employment and maternity rights; child care; education and training opportunities; and family and social security benefits for women. Our Ministry for Women will signal our determination in government to see that, in every area of policy, rights and opportunities of women are strengthened.'

(Neil Kinnock, 25 March 1991, launching the Labour Party's policy document for women)

'I want more women in top posts, but it is just as important that the average woman should have the same scope for development and fulfilment at work as the average man. Relatively few men think that combining career, marriage and children will involve choice or pose dilemmas, but for women these three single human ambitions are still hard to combine. The time has come to ask why women should need to be prepared to conform to traditional working patterns. Why can't work be organized on a part-time basis, with or without job-sharing? Why can't career breaks be recognized as something positive from which people might actually gain in terms of effectiveness and fresh thinking?'

(John Major, 28 October 1991, launching Opportunity 2000, a campaign by business to encourage companies to get women into top jobs)

Creches allow mothers to work.

IN PAIRS

Working arrangements – the flexible approach

Many businesses are developing flexible working patterns to suit employees' other commitments, e.g. their responsibilities for caring for children or disabled or elderly relatives.

Find out about the following: (**a**) job-sharing, (**b**) Term-time working, (**c**) Flexi-time, (**d**) annual hours contract, (**e**) home-based working.

IN GROUPS

Study the article on 'Feminism and Equality', opposite. Discuss what Mya, Sally, Penny and Amanda say in the article about feminism and equality.

What are your views on feminism? What has it achieved? Is it still relevant?

'I got stuck on a junior level

The bank

LESLEY Wayne started as a teagirl for one of the major high street clearing banks at 16. Twenty-two years later, she has, she says, "crawled" into middle management and is one of three managers in a big branch, *writes Madeleine Bunting.*

She is one of a tiny minority; only 6 per cent of the bank's managers are women, yet 57 per cent of its employees are women. It's been an uphill struggle and she is not surprised she has so few women colleagues.

"When I started in the late 1960s, men were paid more for the same job. When a woman married it was presumed she would leave. Women worked in the back office and were only allowed to go on the counters on Saturday mornings as a sort of treat or reward.

"I got stuck in my twenties for six years on a junior clerical level — I'd married and the bank labelled me with the career potential assessment of a married woman — that meant a secretary for life. I went through a grievance procedure for 18 months to get myself reassessed because only then was there any chance of getting the training I needed."

Ms Wayne believes there are far better opportunities for women but as it has taken 20 years to make a bank manager, it will take more than a decade of reforms before a significant number of women reach the top.

The Guardian (29/10/91)

FOR YOUR FILE

If someone was appointed as minister for women, what do you think their top priorities should be? Write a letter to the minister for women saying what you think their priorities should be.

FEMINISM AND EQUALITY

Four young women – Mya, 25 a legal executive, Sally, 23 a student journalist, Penny, 22 a bank clerk and Amanda, 24 an actress – express their views on feminism and equal opportunities.

What does feminism mean to you?	**Mya** Not compromising your values. **Sally** Feminism is about women living as individuals, not being man-orientated and not having marriage as their only goal.	**Amanda** Equality. Feminism is about saying 'I am a woman but I'm also a human being.'
Do you think feminism is outdated?	**Mya** Feminism is about fighting for rights – how can it be outdated? **Sally** Feminism is still very relevant. Women still aren't equal – they don't get top management jobs and often don't get equal pay.	**Amanda** The ideals still need to be worked at, but I don't think it's as hard a fight. We've crossed the first threshold.
Are women their own worst enemies when it comes to equality?	**Mya** A lot of women like security and feel that by standing-up for their rights that they're doing themselves down. They feel guilt too – if their husband has given them a home and housekeeping money they feel they should be grateful.	**Amanda** Some women are afraid of taking responsibility for themselves. Many women like the role of wife and homemaker, partly because it's so inbred as a kid.
So if we underestimate ourselves, where do these problems start?	**Mya** From the home – from Dad coming home and watching telly and Mum cooking and the girl helping wash-up instead of the boy. No wonder men expect the situation to continue when they get a girlfriend. It's social conditioning. Even at school the boys play rugby while the girls play netball. **Sally** It's difficult to say that it's anybody's fault. It's just the way it's always been. It's not men's fault they're brought-up the way they are. It's the way society is.	**Penny** It's always been the attitude that it's more important for boys to get qualifications because girls are just going to get married and have babies. That's the problem – women are always being underestimated. Even at work if a woman does well the first thing anyone says is, 'Who has she slept with?'
How can we change the situation?	**Mya** Women have to have a high profile in everything from industry to the media. Look at parliament – nearly all the MPs are men. It's ridiculous – these people are deciding the future of the country! We've got to make a move there as well. If children grow-up in this sort of environment girls will continue to take a back seat. **Sally** As women change, so will men. If women grow-up knowing they can have their own lives and their own careers, they will go out with men as individuals – and men will learn to respect them as equals. But we have to change the way we mother our children.	**Amanda** There's a lot you can do in your daily life, but the best thing to do would be to teach your children. That's the only way to change things – start with the kids. 
Should there be a Minister for Women?	**Mya** I've got mixed feelings. It's brilliant because you've got someone pioneering for your rights, but it's also a bit patronising. And it might just perpetuate bad feelings about feminism – men will complain that they don't have a Minister for Men.	**Sally** It would be better to have more women MPs because then the causes will be promoted anyway. Having a Minister for Women might be dangerous. A lot of things would be bypassed and just put on the pile for the Minister for Women.

SEXUAL HARASSMENT

The Trades Union Congress define sexual harassment as:

'Repeated and unwanted verbal or sexual advances, sexually explicit derogatory statements . . . which cause the worker to feel threatened, humiliated, patronized or harassed, or which interfere with the worker's job performance, undermine job security or create a threatening or intimidating work environment.'

In October 1991, the Sunday Times surveyed 200 women at work, consisting of 100 top professionals from politics, arts and business and 100 clerical and secretarial staff. A total of 40 per cent said they had been harassed at some point. But they found it hard to agree on what constitutes harassment.

Wolf-whistling, leering and lewd remarks.

Every time I walk past builders I know they will leer and make remarks. In fact, the further up the scaffolding they are, the more offensive they get.

If I walk past building sites and men whistle at me, I just look round and smile at them. I don't find it offensive – I just think they must be bored and have nothing else to do. .

Pin-ups in the office were regarded as unacceptable by seven in 10 professionals, but only four in 10 clerical workers said they constituted harassment. A third of the professionals said flirting could be harassment, while 94% of clericals disagreed.

Four in 10 of the professional women found sexual jokes offensive compared with only 20% of clerical workers. Seven in 10 of the professional group said they felt harassed by pressure from male colleagues to go on dates, while only 60% of clerical staff objected. Both categories were united in finding the discussion of pornography and sexual remarks in an office offensive. More than 75% of both groups of women agreed it constituted sexual harassment.

However, sharp divisions appeared over whether a man placing his arm around a woman amounted to harassment. Nearly six in 10 professional women found it offensive compared with three in 10 clerical staff.

© *Sunday Times* (Oct 1991)

USE YOUR COMMON SENSE, MEN TOLD

By TRACEY HARRISON

JUST putting a friendly arm around a girl at work might seem harmless enough.

But while some women would not think twice about it, many would feel patronised or even sexually harassed, say experts.

Eve Warren, of the Industrial Society's equal opportunities unit said: 'Common sense should tell men what is acceptable.

'The key thing is not to do anything which is obviously unwelcome or causes offence, because if you continue doing it then that becomes harassment.

'You can tell a woman she looks nice, but if you make a comment or innuendo about her appearance which implies she is only there to be looked at, it's a different matter.'

Vivienne Walker, of the Institute of Personal Management, said: 'What one person finds acceptable another doesn't. But if it's clear a woman feels intimidated or small by what you do, then you don't do it again.'

Daily Mail (1/2/91)

IN GROUPS

Study the results of the *Sunday Times* survey. How would you define sexual harassment? Make a list of all the different types of behaviour which you think are examples of sexual harassment.

What do you think should happen to someone who is guilty of harassment? Should they be dismissed, disciplined or warned?

What do you think of wolf-whistling, leering and making lewd remarks in public? Should women be given greater protection from such behaviour?

ROLE PLAY

You are a working-party set up by your company to draw-up a code of conduct for the work-force, explaining what the company's policy is on sexual harassment. Draw up a statement saying what actions you think should be considered as sexual harassment and stating how complaints will be dealt with and what action will be taken against people found guilty of sexual harassment.

PAGE 3 – pornography or harmless fun?

In 1988, Clare Short, MP for Birmingham Ladywood, unsuccessfully tried to introduce a bill to ban Page 3 photos. She believes that the institution of Page 3 is a degrading and damaging one.

'Deeply offensive pictures of naked and semi-naked women in national newspapers should be banned. These topless pictures make women look as if they are available . . . to be used and abused as men wish. That women exist only to be leered at and lusted over. These pictures distort relationships between men and women. And this can lead to men using them, knocking them about and ultimately raping them.'

Yvonne Paul runs one of the most successful glamour model agencies in Britain. She argues that there is absolutely no evidence to link Page 3 with any kind of sexual violence.

'Page 3 is not pornography. Pornography is highly explicit, erotic photography with an editorial to match. It's designed totally to titillate. Page 3 is just a pretty girl with no top on in a newspaper – if that incites someone to commit a violent or sexual attack, then that person is likely to be unstable and should be locked-up. God knows what he'd do surrounded by topless girls on a beach.

I think Clare Short is wasting her time. I wish she'd use her energy to ban something a lot more useful – like banning battery cages.

I suppose the girls on Page 3 and the Page 7 fellas are sexual objects but Marilyn Monroe and Robert Redford were sexual objects. We've always had pin-ups, there's nothing wrong with them.'

Rachel Garley is 21 and has been a topless model for five years. She appears regularly on Page 3 and is proud of her career.

'I don't think I'm being exploited at all. I believe in letting people do whatever they want to do. People don't have to read newspapers with naked women in them. It's like boxing – I don't like it, but I'm not out to ban it, am I? Page 3 doesn't degrade women. I like doing it. I'm not embarrassed by doing it.

Page 3 doesn't cause rape. On the contrary, I think it prevents it. If it was banned I think there would be more trouble.'

Mizz (Issue 143)

The Campaign Against Pornography

The Campaign Against Pornography has three aims:

1 To introduce legislation against pornography, including Page 3 on the grounds that it degrades, damages and disadvantages women.

2 To publish evidence of the ways that women suffer as a result of pornography.

3 To mobilize women nationally in the campaign, with letters to their MPs and the media and direct action against the distributors of porn, e.g. 'off-the-shelf' campaigns in which women take magazines from the shelves and talk about it with the manager/manageress of the newsagents.

IN GROUPS

Why does Clare Short object to Page 3? What arguments in defence of Page 3 do Yvonne Paul and Rachel Garley put forward?

Whose arguments do you find more convincing – those in favour of Page 3 or those against it?

Do you think pornography encourages violence against women? If you were an MP would you vote for or against a law banning all pornography?

IN PAIRS

Discuss your views of glamour modelling as a career. What do you think of women who pose topless or nude? Are they allowing themselves to be exploited? What advice would you give to a friend who is thinking of becoming a glamour model? Would you try to encourage her or discourage her?

FOR YOUR FILE

Write an article for a teenage magazine's *In my opinion* page stating your views on Page 3, glamour modelling and pornography.

Shopping and the law

Whenever you buy something, you and the seller are making a contract. A contract involves three things:

- **The offer** – you offer to buy the goods.
- **The acceptance** – the seller accepts your offer for the goods.
- **Consideration** – your payment, or your promise to pay, the agreed price in exchange for the goods.

The contract you make with the seller can be oral or written and it is legally binding. Because you make a contract with the seller rather than the manufacturer, it is the seller who has to sort things out if you have a complaint.

Your rights when you buy goods are protected by certain laws.

The Sale of Goods Act, 1979

This is a civil law. It applies to all new and second-hand goods (including goods bought in sales), whether you buy them in a shop, in a street market, from a mail order catalogue or from a door-to-door salesperson. The law has three rules:

1 The goods must be of *merchantable quality*. This means they must not be faulty and must be reasonably fit for their normal purpose. New items must not be broken or damaged and must work properly.

2 Goods must be *fit for any particular purpose* which you have explained to the seller. For example, the scissors you buy for dressmaking must be sharp enough to cut cloth.

3 Goods must be *as described*. A leather belt for example, must be leather and not plastic.

These three rules apply to all goods you buy from a trader. But if you buy goods from a private individual, you have fewer rights. The Sale of Goods Act, 1979 says that all goods sold privately only have to match their description.

The Supply of Goods and Services Act, 1982

This is a civil law which extends your rights under the Sale of Goods Act to any goods or materials provided as part of a service or on hire. It also states rules about the supply of services (see page 14).

Consumer Protection Act, 1987

This act contains both civil laws and criminal laws and protects you in three ways:

1 It makes the manufacturer or importer of a defective product liable for any loss or damage caused by the product. In other words, if you buy a product that is defective because it falls below the standard of safety you are entitled to expect, you can claim compensation for any personal injury or damages that it causes.

2 It makes it a criminal offence for a trader to sell unsafe goods. There are specific safety regulations for certain goods, such as toys and pushchairs.

3 It is an offence for a trader to give consumers a misleading indication about the price of goods or services.

The Trades Description Act, 1968

This is a criminal law which makes it illegal for traders to make false statements about the goods they are selling.

The Weights and Measures Act, 1985

This makes it a criminal offence to sell short weights or measures.

The Food Safety Act, 1990

This is a criminal law, carrying severe penalties for anyone convicted of selling food that fails to comply with food safety requirements or misleading the buyer about the nature, substance or quality of the food.

The Office of Fair Trading

This is a government department based in London. Its job is to protect the consumer by making sure that trading practices are as fair as possible and by encouraging competition.

Consumer Protection/Trading Standards Departments

They investigate local cases of inaccurate weights and measures, false or misleading descriptions of goods and certain aspects of the safety of goods. The consumer protection laws give them wide powers to prosecute traders who break the law.

Environmental Health Departments

These are council departments who enforce certain laws concerning health matters, such as food safety regulations.

IN GROUPS

In groups discuss each of the situations described in the section 'What should I do?' What are the person's rights? What would you advise them to do? Appoint someone in the group to act as spokesperson and report your views to the rest of the class in a class discussion.

ROLE PLAY

In pairs, choose one of the situations described in the section 'What should I do?' and develop a role play in which the buyer asks for their money back. Do the scene twice. First, show the person complaining in a loud, rude, aggressive manner. Then, show them making their complaint politely, but assertively.

FOR YOUR FILE

Imagine that you bought an item of sports equipment which turned out to be faulty and that the shop is refusing to give you a refund. Write a letter of complaint to the Customer Services Manager/Manageress, saying where and when you bought it and what the fault is, describing what action you have taken to try to get them to put matters right and what exactly you want them to do – refund your money, replace the item or repair it.

What should I do?

A I bought a camera and the second time I used it the shutter jammed. The shopkeeper said it was my fault for not taking enough care with it. The shopkeeper said that they would have to send it back to the manufacturer and that I'd have to pay for the repair.

B I bought this furry toy for my baby brother. When he began to play with it the head came off and he cut his hand on a sharp piece of metal inside.

C I bought this jumper to go with my track suit trousers. When I got home, I found it was the wrong colour.

D My friend gave me a box of chocolates for my birthday. When I opened them, I found the soft centres had leaked everywhere.

E I bought a pair of jeans marked as having a 30″ waist from a market stall. But they must have been wrongly sized, because they were far too tight. When I took them back, the stallholder said it was my fault for buying the wrong size.

F I bought a watch from a friend. After a week it stopped. My friend refuses either to give me my money back or pay to get it repaired.

G I bought a briefcase in a sale at a second-hand shop. When I got it home, I found the catch wouldn't work properly. They are refusing to change it because it was a sale item.

H I was given a make-up bag for my birthday by my aunt. She told me where she bought it, so I could change it if I didn't like it. But the shop say they won't change it, because I don't have a receipt.

If you want a refund . . .

1 You don't have to have the receipt. Proof of purchase can be something like the shop's label or price tag.

2 You don't have to accept a credit note, replacement or repair. You are entitled to a refund, if that's what you want.

3 You don't have to allow the shop to send the goods back to the manufacturer for them to agree that they are faulty.

4 Ignore any signs which say 'No refunds', because such signs are illegal.

But you must have a proper reason for wanting a refund. You can't demand a refund just because you have changed your mind.

A satisfactory service?

When you ask a person or a company to do something for you and agree to pay them, you are buying a service. Some typical services are hairdressers, dry cleaners, garages – and anyone you ask to repair something of yours, such as a tape-deck, a bike or a watch.

When you are buying a service, you are buying a skill. So there are laws to protect you against shoddy work, faulty goods or unreasonable charges.

The Supply of Goods and Services Act, 1982 (see page 12) states that:

1 Anyone providing a service should do so with reasonable skill and care. The service must be carried out to a proper standard. For example, if you ask a hairdresser for blonde highlights, you should not end up with orange streaks because the colour was applied incorrectly.

2 A job should also be done within a reasonable time. But if you and the supplier agree on a completion date, you can't complain unless they fail to meet the deadline.

3 The charge for the service should be reasonable. You can decide if you think a price is reasonable by comparing it to the price charged by other traders for that particular service. You can complain if you think the cost is too high – unless, of course, you agreed a price before the supplier started work.

The Supply of Goods and Services Act does not apply in Scotland. But people in Scotland have similar rights under common law.

If you have a complaint . . .

Take the matter up with the supplier. If that doesn't work, then contact either your local Consumer Protection (or Trading Standards) Department, the Citizens Advice Bureau or the Consumer Advice Centre and ask for advice.

Letters about unsatisfactory services

1 Explain your complaint:
- describe the service
- say when it was done
- say how much it cost
- state what was wrong with it, with evidence if possible.

2 Describe what action you've taken:
- say whether you complained at the time and to whom
- say if you've done anything else.

3 Describe what you want the firm to do:
- say whether you want the job put right
- state whether you want a refund and/or compensation.

IN PAIRS

Problems with services

Discuss these problems. What are the person's rights? What would you advise each of them to do?

- I took my jacket in for repair and they said that it would take about two weeks. It took them six weeks, and when it came back you could still see where it had been torn.

- The cost of repairing the clasp on my bracelet was twice what I thought it would be, but they refused to give it back until I paid.

- I hired this bicycle and paid a £10 deposit. While I was riding it, the chain snapped. When I asked for a refund and for my deposit back, they refused and accused me of being responsible for breaking the chain.

Estimates and quotations

An estimate tells you approximately what the cost of the service will be. The actual price depends on exactly what work has to be done and how long it takes. So the final cost could be more or less than the estimate.

A quotation tells you the exact price you will have to pay. It is part of the contract between you and the person providing the service.

FOR YOUR FILE

Write to a firm who repaired your stereo complaining that the final cost was twice the estimated charge, that it still doesn't work and it now has several large scratches on it that were not there before. Follow the guidelines for letter-writing, given on this page, and make sure the tone of your letter is firm but polite.

Mail Order

Buying by post can be a convenient way of shopping and most transactions are completed satisfactorily. But what happens if things go wrong? What are your rights?

The Office of Fair Trading suggests seven golden rules for you to follow whenever you buy by post (see right).

Golden Rules

Here are seven golden rules to follow before you buy by post.

1 Check that the newspaper, magazine, or catalogue is up-to-date.

2 If you buy through a newspaper or magazine advert check whether you're covered by a protection scheme (see page 3). If you're not, and you pay in advance, you could lose your money if the trader goes bust.

3 If you have to send money never send *cash* by post. Use cheques or postal orders, and make sure you retain cheque stubs or counterfoils as a record of your payment. If a large sum of money is involved, use recorded delivery.

4 When you write (and when you return goods) always include your name and address.

5 Keep a copy of your order and note the date it was sent.

6 Keep a copy of the advert. If this isn't possible keep a note of the name and address of the advertiser, where and when the advert appeared and any other details such as charges for postage and packing and the time to allow for delivery.

7 If you have a complaint make sure you give full details of your order and of the advert.

Can I get my money back?

If goods are faulty or wrongly described, you are entitled to all or some of your money back. It depends on what the fault is and how long you have had the goods.

If you insist on a delivery date when you send for the goods and it isn't met, you can cancel your order and ask for your money back. Even if you don't give a definite date the seller has to deliver within a reasonable time. If he doesn't, write or phone saying that if the goods haven't arrived by a certain date – say, within two weeks – you won't want them and you will want your money back. But if you agree to give them extra time – say, another month – you can't change your mind and try to cancel your order before that time is up.

Buying from a catalogue

Many companies which sell through catalogues belong to the Mail Order Traders' Association (MOTA) which follows a Code of Practice. Look for their symbol. Their catalogues refer to the Code and tell you how to complain.

Buying books and tapes

Many firms which sell books or tapes belong to the Association of Mail Order Publishers (AMOP). The Association has a Code of Practice to protect customers. The Code requires members to ensure that information about quantity, quality, price and terms of business is given accurately. As a member of a club you will have a contract. With a 'series', you can normally cancel after 12 months or at any time if prices rise more than expected.

Buying from a newspaper or magazine advert

Most large magazines and newspapers belong to a mail order protection scheme. So, if you send money to an advertiser who goes out of business before the goods arrive, the advertising manager of the newspaper or magazine should arrange a refund. The scheme does not apply, however, if you have ordered from a catalogue or an advert which appeared in the classified columns.

IN GROUPS

List the advantages and disadvantages of mail order shopping. Discuss the problems these teenagers are having. What are their rights? What would you advise them to do?

I ordered a blouse for my mum's birthday from a magazine. The ad said to allow four weeks for delivery, but it took nine weeks, so I didn't get it in time. Can I send it back and demand a refund? (Tina)

I sent off for a bracelet that was on offer in the newspaper. It never arrived and eventually we found out that the firm who supplied it had gone bust. What can I do to get my money back? (Netta)

I joined this club which offered cheap tapes. They keep on sending me tapes I don't want every month. My friend says there's nothing I can do, it's my fault for joining in the first place. Is she right? (Jay)

I sent off for a book and when it arrived I found they'd added an extra £2 for postage and packing. Can they do this? (Gordon)

I ordered a sports bag from a catalogue and, now that I've got it, I don't like the colour. Can I send it back? (Mark)

Pre-Menstrual Syndrome

What is Pre-Menstrual Syndrome?

Most women can anticipate the onset of a period. They may feel a little tetchy, have slight breast tenderness and suffer with spots. These minor irritations are perfectly normal.

A PMS sufferer's symptoms are far more exaggerated and difficult to live with. Some women find that the syndrome plays havoc with a large part of their lives and that they are only free of symptoms for one week out of every month.

Symptoms fall into two groups – physical and psychological.

Physically, the sufferer may experience some or all of the following symptoms – bloating; aching breasts; weight gain; fluid retention; severe headaches; fatigue; clumsiness and food cravings, especially for sweet things.

Psychological symptoms include depression; irritability; lack of concentration; feeling violent; tearfulness and loss of memory. The most important factor in diagnosing PMS is to determine when these symptoms arise. If a woman suffers these symptoms persistently, it's unlikely they're related to PMS. Obviously, any of the above symptoms can be linked to other illnesses. To be diagnosed as a PMS sufferer the following must apply:

- Symptoms must occur after ovulation (release of egg from ovary) and before the start of menstruation (period).

- The symptoms must totally disappear after the start of menstruation and not return for at least 7 days.

- Symptoms must occur every month.

From this we can see that PMS sufferers will have symptoms every month, starting anything up to two weeks before the beginning of a period. Symptoms will disappear completely with the onset of bleeding, with complete relief for *at least*

An estimated 50 per cent of women of child-bearing age suffer from Pre-Menstrual Syndrome. Around 15 per cent of these women experience particularly bad symptoms.

one week. Period pain mustn't be confused with PMS and isn't defined as one of the ailments associated with it.

A good way of working out if you have PMS is to draw up a 28-day chart listing all the symptoms. From day one of starting the chart, log if you have any symptoms and mark the severity with a code, i.e. N for None, M for Mild, B for Bad and S for Severe. Then remember to mark the day you start your period with P. From this chart you'll be able to work out your own pattern of symptoms and see if you suffer from PMS.

What causes PMS?

According to Nick Siddle, consultant obstetrician and gynaecologist at University College Hospital, London, there are around 20 different theories as to what causes PMS. The most widely held belief – and a belief held by Siddle himself – is that PMS is caused by an imbalance of hormones during the second half of the menstrual cycle. This would explain why symptoms occur within the two weeks leading up to menstruation.

Dr Katharina Dalton, widely acclaimed for her research into PMS, is convinced that a lack of progesterone is responsible for the condition. Again, it is progesterone which is produced during the second half of the cycle. Why one woman produces sufficient amounts of the hormone to be free of symptoms and another doesn't, isn't clearly known. Indeed, PMS continues to be a complaint to which there are no steadfast medical answers.

Coping with PMS

There is no one single treatment that works for everyone who suffers from PMS. The first thing to do is to consult your doctor. Sometimes just establishing that it's PMS that's responsible for your mood swings is a real help.

The doctor will probably suggest you try a special diet. Many women find that their well-being improves dramatically as a result. Your progress will be carefully monitored by your doctor and, if appropriate, they may prescribe some hormone supplements as well. Some women find that taking vitamin B6 helps to reduce the severity of the symptoms. But don't start taking it unless your doctor suggests it, as taking too much can have side-effects. It's wise to consult your doctor, before trying any home remedies.

Jenny's story

Jenny, aged 16, describes how recognizing that she suffered from PMS and consulting her doctor helped to change her life. 'At first I tried a special diet that has been proven to help around 60 per cent of women who suffer from PMS. I still stick to it even now, but unfortunately I was one of those who needed to take some hormone tablets too, to help the process along. I don't have to eat anything different to what I would normally have had, but instead I break-up my routine so that I have six small meals instead of the normal three. This stops my blood sugar level from dropping too much and making me feel lethargic.

I feel an awful lot better now and the dark moods I had are a thing of the past. I really can't describe how I felt before I started this treatment. It was like being a Jekyll and Hyde. Sometimes I would sit in a class by myself quietly sobbing, then the following day I would be everyone's friend again and I'd be dying to have a laugh with my mates. I'm so glad that I managed to sort it out.

I honestly believe that tons of women in this country suffer from PMS of some kind, even if it is only a mild form. Most people don't realize it exists, or just refer to it as pre-menstrual tension – something totally normal that they can't do anything about. They should realize that there is a lot they can do to change the situation.'

Mizz (Issue 177)

Dear Alex,
Please help me. I get these terrible mood swings. Sometimes I feel great and everything's going fine, at other times I get so irritable that if the slightest thing goes wrong then I fly off the handle. Physically, it's the same. On good days, I feel full of energy. On bad days, I get headaches and feel so lethargic all I want to do is stay in bed all day. Someone said it's probably due to my menstrual cycle and I'll just have to learn to live with it. Are they right?
Marlene

Rebecca's story

Rebecca, 21, suffers from PMS

'Knowingly, I've been a sufferer for four years. My periods started when I was 13 but no-one has records back that far as to how obnoxious I was!

I tend to have symptoms every month, but some months are worse than others. Suddenly it hits me and I feel absolutely awful. I shout at my boyfriend for no reason and then I realize – it's *that* time of the month. Physically, everything swells – especially around my stomach, and my breasts ache so much that it's difficult to have a cuddle. I get spotty and I develop a real craving for chocolate.

Psychologically, I feel really depressed and the slightest thing makes me cry. The other day I went to pour a drink and I missed the glass and dropped the carton. I got so upset I swore and rushed out of the kitchen and slammed the door. I know that sounds irrational but that's exactly how you feel when you've got PMS. But as soon as the period starts all the symptoms disappear.

Luckily my boyfriend knows I suffer and he makes allowances for it. I react far more sensitively to things he says. Even when he says something quite jokey about my behaviour I fly off the handle.

When I'm pre-menstrual all I want to do is lie in bed, but the reality is I've got to get on with my life. I went to the doctor the other day and I was really glad that I made the effort. She was really understanding and suggested I take vitamin B6 for a few months. I'll see how I get on. At least I'm not in the dark any more. It helps to talk to someone about it – it makes you realize you're not alone and you're not going barmy.'

Adapted from *Just Seventeen*

IN PAIRS

Study the information on these pages, then draft a reply to Marlene's letter.

In your reply try to explain to Marlene what Pre-Menstrual Syndrome is, what is believed to be the cause of Pre-Menstrual Syndrome, how it can affect the lives of women who suffer from it, and what action she could take to cope with it better.

Look after your skin

During puberty many adolescents get acne – spots on their skin. They are caused by the changes in hormone levels in your body.

Almost every teenage boy and about 50 per cent of girls suffer at least a mild form of acne at some time in their teens. Boys tend to have more problems because they have more of the hormone testosterone, which is more commonly involved with the formation of spots.

What causes acne?

There are many myths about the causes of acne. It isn't caused by not washing properly or by eating too many fatty foods or too much chocolate. Nor is it an infection that you can catch. Also, there's no medical evidence to link it to stress and nervousness, although the symptoms of acne may cause anxiety and depression.

Acne is caused when the sebaceous glands in your skin start producing too much sebum – an oily substance which keeps your skin soft and waterproof. As a result, the sebaceous gland outlet – the skin pore – becomes plugged with sebum. Since there are a large number of these glands in your face, neck and back, that's where acne occurs.

What can you do about acne?

Make sure that you keep your skin clean by washing carefully twice a day. But remember that acne is not a sign of dirtiness and that too much washing can harm the skin and make the acne worse.

Ask your chemist for advice about which creams to use. But if you are one of the thousands of teenagers whose acne doesn't seem to clear up, or gets worse, consult your doctor. There are several ointments doctors can prescribe and they may put you on a course of antibiotics. But don't expect results overnight. Successful treatment takes months rather than weeks.

'My skin developed acne when I was 14. For 10 years, I tried every product under the sun because I felt too ashamed to tell my doctor about it. Finally I made an appointment to see her and she put me on a course of mild antibiotics and prescribed an ointment containing benzoyl peroxide. It must have been three months before I started to see any real improvement, but at least that broke the vicious circle of picking, which had been making my skin even worse. After about a year, my skin was practically clear. It was a revelation really. I felt I could face people without an inch-thick layer of foundation.'

(Ex-acne sufferer)

IN PAIRS

Study the information on this page and decide which of the following statements are true and which are false.

A Acne is contagious.

B Even severe acne can be successfully treated.

C Acne sufferers should wash five times a day.

D You can cure acne by eating a special diet.

E There is no link between nervousness and tension and an outbreak of spots.

F Boys are more likely to suffer from acne than girls.

G Acne can be cured very quickly.

H Acne will go away in a year or so, if you leave it alone.

Sunbathing is relaxing, but take care – particularly if you have fair skin. The ultra-violet rays in sunlight can cause long-term damage to your skin and can even cause skin cancer.

Tattoos

Robert Leedham, The *Guardian* (14/1/92)

Terry Marr loves her tattoos. She has a dove on her shoulder and a band of roses around her left wrist. 'I think they look great,' she says. 'Everybody thinks they look sexy.'

At 15, Terry is one of the growing number of young people, especially girls, choosing to get tattooed. Tattooing is suddenly fashionable again, promoted by celebrities such as Madonna and Cher.

The sixth World Tattoo Expo was recently held in Dunstable, Bedfordshire, attracting 5,000 visitors, many young.

Tattooing is considered an art form in many cultures and the electronic tattooing machine celebrated its 100th anniversary last month. But the professional tattooing of under-18s has been illegal in Britain since 1969. The law was introduced after it was discovered that the average age for those being tattooed was 16. Yet it seems little has changed since the sixties.

Dr Patrick Hall-Smith runs a tattoo-removal clinic in the Plastic Surgery Unit of Brighton General Hospital. He recently surveyed his patients and found the average age for receiving a professional tattoo to be 16. Those who apply their own are about 15 – but non-professionals who use unsterilized needles may be at risk of transmitting HIV or other serious diseases.

'It's a tragedy,' he says. 'My patients bitterly regret their tattoos. The boys have a few drinks, get pushed into a tattoo parlour and come out with their lives ruined. Tattoos are a socio-economic disaster: you won't get a job in a bank with 'Love' and 'Hate' on your knuckles.'

Increasingly, Dr Hall-Smith is seeing people who want to lose their tattoos – two-thirds of them women. But tattoos are notoriously difficult, often impossible, to remove despite the use of skin grafts, acids and lasers.

'I've been coming for six years,' says Sharon Hart, now 27, 'and the process is pretty horrific. The acid burns right into your skin. The holes always go septic.'

Sharon holds out an upper arm that looks like gorgonzola cheese 'I was 15 – my friends were bikers and we all wanted tattoos. One's a dragon, one's a parrot, one's a sailor's sea grave and one is a devil. They've cut off the jobs I wanted and ruined my marriage.'

Tania Brown agrees that tattoos can complicate life. 'You get looked at like a freak. You go paranoid and stop going to the beach,' she says. 'I was 18 and someone said, 'You ain't got the bottle.' So I had a swallow and a butterfly done on my left arm, a flower and a devil on my right. But if I'd have known then how much hassle they would be, I'd never have got them done.'

Dr Hall-Smith is campaigning for the law to be changed. He wants a compulsory 'cooling-off-period' between ordering a tattoo and actually having it applied so that people do not do so on impulse.

This would not have stopped Terry Marr. 'I'm proud of them. I want another one soon. But I haven't quite decided what design I want yet.'

IN GROUPS

Why do people have tattoos done? Would you ever consider having a tattoo?

Why is it risky to tattoo yourself or to let a non-professional tattoo you?

Why do many people who have themselves tattooed eventually regret it?

What do you think of people who have tattoos?

Do you think the law about tattooing should be changed in any way?

ROLE PLAY

In pairs, act out a scene in which a person in their twenties, who regrets having had tattoos, explains why to a teenager. In groups, act out a scene in which three young people try to pressurize someone into having a tattoo that they don't really want. Take it in turns to be the person who doesn't want to be tattooed. Then, discuss the reasons each person gave for refusing to have a tattoo. Which of you managed to resist the pressure most effectively? Talk about why.

FOR YOUR FILE

'I wish I'd never had it done.' Write a story about a person who got themselves tattooed and then regretted it.

THIRD WORLD

What are the effects of urbanization?

Many cities are growing so fast that it is impossible to provide homes and to develop transport, water and sanitation systems fast enough to meet the needs of the people arriving from rural areas. There are not enough jobs and the migrants are forced to fend for themselves as best they can. Many of them live in poverty in squatter settlements on the edge of the cities.

The larger a city grows, the more waste it produces. As well as the problems of refuse disposal, there is also the problem of air pollution from increased traffic.

Urbanization – the growth of towns and cities – is taking place in every country of the world. In 1960 there were only 114 cities in the world with over 1 million inhabitants – including 25 in Western Europe, 52 in the Third World. By 1980 the number had risen to 222 – 32 in Western Europe and 119 in the Third World. So urbanization is taking place very rapidly in the Third World.

The United Nations predicts that by the year 2000 there will be 60 metropolitan areas with 4 million or more inhabitants. Only a quarter of these 'super-cities' will be in the industrial nations. The other 45 will be in the less developed countries.

What causes urbanization in the Third World?

- Changes in the way rural land is used and owned have *pushed* unemployed and landless rural workers into towns and cities, without necessarily producing more food for urban people. Today's new large-scale mechanized farms are often set-up to grow produce for export, not to grow food for home markets.

- Changes from traditional to mechanized ways of producing goods and investment in city-related developments have *pulled* labour towards urban centres. But many towns and cities have still not been able to create the jobs and homes that the migrants need. Most of the urban poor have to

create their own work and their own homes.

- Improved communications systems, from mass media to roads and railways, have enabled people to be more mobile and knowledgeable about the possibilities that exist. This has helped *pull* people towards the towns.

- The population explosion has *pushed* people towards towns. In some countries the pressure of people living on the land has become so great that many people have been forced to move to towns.

URBANIZATION

Urban life or rural life – which would you choose?

It is estimated that every day in Third World countries 75,000 people from rural areas migrate to towns.

The bright lights of Bombay versus the tranquillity of village life?

IN GROUPS

If you had the choice of living in a city or a village, which would you choose? On your own, study the arguments for city life and village life. Decide which you would choose, then share your reasons in a group discussion. Do you feel your reasons are likely to be similar to those of someone living in a Third World society?

ARGUMENTS FOR CITY LIFE

The cost of living in cities may be higher, but you'll earn more. In Bangladesh, urban income per person is roughly three times as high as rural income. Most people who choose city life do so for economic reasons. Growing rural populations, people being made landless, lack of employment, and the difficulty of sustaining a decent income from the land are among the reasons people move to the cities.

Although there are health hazards, if you fall ill your chances of getting medical attention are much higher in cities than in rural areas. In Ethiopia, for example, you are three times more likely to be seen by a doctor in Addis Ababa than you would be outside the city.

You have much more chance of getting an education in a city than in a rural area. Education facilities are always better equipped, better staffed and easier to get into than those in rural areas. In Kenya, for example, 85 per cent of children around the capital Nairobi have access to primary education; elsewhere in Kenya as few as 35 per cent do.

The governments of many Third World countries are biased towards urban centres. In countries like Tanzania the majority of investment goes into the 'modern' industrial sectors. Not only can city life convey all sorts of economic and social advantages, it can seem more interesting and dynamic and offer access to new lifestyles and consumer goods. Rural life is dull by comparison. Towns are where the action is.

ARGUMENTS FOR VILLAGE LIFE

If your family has land or there are jobs available locally you may be better off in a village, as employment prospects can be limited in towns and cities. Even though incomes tend to be higher in urban areas, at least 50 per cent of urban dwellers are living in conditions of extreme poverty and are unable to meet basic dietary and other needs. Many people scrape a living somehow. Others turn to begging, prostitution, drug-pushing or petty theft.

You'll be more likely to have a roof over your head. In many cities, 30–60 per cent of the population live in squatter areas or on the pavements.

There are serious health hazards in many cities, because in the squatter settlements you may have inadequate access to clean water and proper sanitation. There is also the problem of waste disposal. For example, around 80 per cent of the houses around Lagos Lagoon have no public refuse disposal. Although cities may be more exciting, they may also be more dangerous. Crime and violence rates in cities generally appear to be higher, as do stresses on family relationships and mental health.

Even where rural life has been disrupted by changes in land use and ownership there can still be a strong sense of community. Rural dwellers experiencing hardship may be able to share food and other resources with family members and friends, something city dwellers may not be able to do.

BRITAIN'S CITIES

INNER CITY DECAY AND URBAN SPRAWL

Many of our cities are old and have, therefore, suffered from urban decay, particularly near the city centre. Crumbling buildings and dereliction are not only unsightly but also influence firms when they are choosing sites for their businesses, and individuals when they are deciding where to live. Firms are less attracted to run-down areas and have, in recent years, increasingly been seeking 'green field sites' which have the additional advantage of offering adequate open spaces so often sought by manufacturing firms. Individuals, especially as incomes have been rising, have tended to move out to suburbia where there is greater security, and the environment is more pleasant. Firms and people have moved from city centres to the suburbs leading to the joint problems of inner city decay and urban sprawl. Neither the city nor the rural environment gain when excessive drifts of this kind occur.

Adapted from *The Urban Environment*, Kenneth Button

Many city centres have been redeveloped in recent years. Old buildings have been demolished and replaced by shopping malls and pedestrian precincts.

In 1981, there were a series of riots in inner city areas, such as Brixton in London, Toxteth in Liverpool and Moss Side in Manchester. One of the causes of the rioting was believed to be inner city decay. Over the next ten years, the Conservative government tried to provide incentives to encourage business and industry to invest in urban renewal schemes. However, progress in redeveloping Britain's inner cities was hampered during the early 1990s by the recession and further riots occurred in many cities throughout Britain.

IN PAIRS

Study the information on this page.

What is meant by urban decay? Are there any areas in your town/city which are suffering from urban decay?

What is meant by urban sprawl? Why has it occurred?

How have many cities centres changed in recent years?

Are there any areas locally which have benefited from urban renewal schemes?

FOR YOUR FILE

Imagine you live in a run-down inner city area. The government has announced that it is going to spend £1000 million on urban renewal schemes in ten top priority areas. Write a letter saying why you think your area should be one of the top ten.

Small blocks of flats which stand in their own grounds have lower crime rates than large blocks.

Blocks of flats with large numbers of dwellings linked by overhead walkways have higher crime rates and more social problems.

IN PAIRS

You are members of a 'think tank'. Your job is to make suggestions as to how to redevelop inner city sites. Study the information on this page and list the design features that planners should include in new estates in order to try to ensure that they do not become 'problem' estates.

IN GROUPS

Discuss these questions on vandalism, then choose a spokesperson to report your ideas to the rest of the class.

What causes vandalism? Why is there often more vandalism in inner city areas than in suburban or rural areas? What different types of vandalism are there? Can vandalism be dangerous as well as costly?

What is your attitude towards graffiti writing? Does it depend on whose property is being defaced? Is defacing community property less serious than defacing private property?

Imagine you saw someone carrying out an act of vandalism, what would you do? Would you tell the police? Do nothing? Why?

If vandals are caught, how do you think they should be treated? If you were a magistrate, what punishments would you give to someone convicted of vandalism?

What can be done to stop vandalism? Discuss how you would run a campaign to try to cut down the amount of vandalism.

URBAN DESIGN AND CRIME

Although billions of pounds have been spent on redeveloping inner cities, many of them still remain problem areas. There is evidence to suggest that there is a link between the design and layout of modern estates and the amount of crime and social breakdown that occurs on them.

A study of over 4,000 blocks of flats found that there was more vandalism and crime and more family breakdowns in large blocks of flats (over three-storeys high, containing thirteen or more dwellings) than there was in small blocks of flats.

Other significant features are the types of entrances, the position of entrances and how the entrances are connected. There is less crime and vandalism where there are ground floor doors with front gardens and where the entrances face the road, than where there are doors not fronted by individual gardens and where the entrances face the interior of the estate.

The study also found that there is more crime where there are overhead walkways and where there are inter-connected entrances. These provide criminals with a variety of routes to get into and out of the block.

The study also found that there are more problems on sites with two or more blocks of flats and more than one gap or gate in the site perimeter.

Altering the design has helped to improve conditions on some estates. For example, when four walkways were removed on one estate, the burglary rate dropped by 55 per cent. On two London estates, the provision of separate front gardens for ground-floor flats helped to improve children's behaviour and bring an end to racial harassment. On another estate, building a wall to create separate grounds for one individual block solved the problems of litter and graffiti.

What is prejudice?

Prejudice is pre-judging a person or a group of people without knowledge, reason, thought or fact. It can mean condemning someone before you know anything about them. This unfair judgement may be because of their colour, sex, age, sexual orientation or religion or perhaps because of their appearance or the way they speak.

Encountering prejudice is always unpleasant. But when whole groups of people have the power to exercise their prejudices it becomes a serious problem. In this unit we will be dealing with racial prejudice and prejudice against homosexuals.

Racism

When racial prejudice is used by people in some form of authority it is known as racism.

Racism is bound up with the way a whole society works – the ethnic majority of a society have power over the ethnic minority.

Institutions or organizations such as schools, workplaces, local and central government, have a powerful position in society. Together they can determine how we live, develop and progress. In a society where racism exists, those in control can intentionally discriminate against and disadvantage people because they belong to a different race – for example, by denying them decent housing, police protection or political power.

The racial balance in Britain

The majority of Britain's population (94.3 per cent) are white. The remainder (5.7 per cent) come from various ethnic backgrounds. But, when it comes to influential jobs, people from ethnic minorities make up far less than this 5.7 per cent. They are under-represented, not only in Parliament, but in senior positions in other key areas such as the law, the civil service and the armed forces.

In 1992, of Britain's 651 MPs only six – Diane Abbott, Paul Boateng, Bernie Grant, Nirj Deva, Piara Chabra and Keith Vas – were from ethnic minorities. If Parliament was truly representative of the population of Britain then there would be 37 MPs from ethnic minorities. Similarly, there are only 3 circuit judges from ethnic minorities – rather than 26, which would be a fairer number.

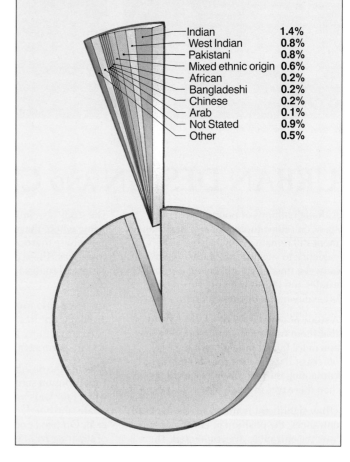

Indian	1.4%
West Indian	0.8%
Pakistani	0.8%
Mixed ethnic origin	0.6%
African	0.2%
Bangladeshi	0.2%
Chinese	0.2%
Arab	0.1%
Not Stated	0.9%
Other	0.5%

RACIAL PREJUDICE **POWER** **RACISM**

EQUAL BEFORE THE LAW?

● Home Office statistics show that the proportion of ethnic minority remand prisoners eventually acquitted, or not proceeded against, is twice as high as that of white remand prisoners. Yet ethnic minority people are more likely to be remanded in custody than white people.

CROWN COURT

CRE PUBLICATIONS ON THE CRIMINAL JUSTICE SYSTEM

★ Bail Hostels and Racial Equality (£1.00)
★ The Criminal Justice System (England and Wales); A role for Community Relations Councils and other voluntary organisations (£1.50)
★ Juvenile Cautioning and Ethnic Monitoring (£1.00)
★ Racial Equality and the Prison Service; The case for training (£1.00)
★ Racial Justice in Magistrates Courts; The case for training (£1.00)

Please add 10% for post and packing and make cheques/postal orders payable to the **COMMISSION FOR RACIAL EQUALITY**
Send to CRE, Elliot House, 10-12 Allington St. London SW1E 5EH (☎ 071-828 7022).

EQUAL JUSTICE FOR ALL

Racism's smiling face unmasked

THE ONE THING that surprised Vas Patel was how pleasant people were to his face when they were being racist and bigoted, **writes Heather Mills.**

"I would leave the accommodation agency, possibly empty-handed, but believing everything had been done to help me in my search. It was only when my white partner went in and was offered more choice of accommodation or places in different areas that I realised people had been affected by the colour of my skin," he said. "I felt hurt. It was all so subtle."

Mr Patel, 28, was one of the men and women from minority ethnic groups employed by the Commission for Racial Equality to test for discrimination in the private rented housing sector. He spent several weeks suffering this hidden discrimination as he visited estate agencies, letting agencies, landlords and landladies, guest houses and small hotels.

"It was a dehumanising experience. I now question how much subtle racism is taking place all the time. It is not so easy to take people at face value."

The Independent (14/9/90)

Figures for 1989 suggest that about 16 per cent of the 48,000 people in prison were from ethnic minorities, when those groups accounted for only 4.6 per cent of the general population. For people on remand, the figure was 21 per cent; a quarter of all remanded women were black. More than 11 per cent of all prisoners were Afro-Caribbean, when they represented only 1 to 2 per cent of the population.

The Independent (11/10/90)

EMPLOYERS are still guilty of deep-seated racial discrimination, a report says today.

It remains despite millions of pounds of Government grants to fight prejudice.

Blacks are twice as likely to be unemployed as whites, according to the report commissioned by the Home Office.

Daily Mail (7/6/91)

THE CODE SPELLS IT OUT

Racial discrimination is a harsh reality. Now there is a statutory code which tells you what the law is, how to avoid inequality in housing, and how to deal with racial harassment.

The code is available from the
COMMISSION FOR RACIAL EQUALITY,
Elliot House, 10-12 Allington St.
London SW1E 5EH.
☎ 071-828 7022

EQUALITY IN HOUSING

COMMISSION FOR RACIAL EQUALITY

IN PAIRS

What is the difference between (**a**) prejudice and racism, (**b**) racial discrimination and racial harassment?

What is meant by institutional racism?

IN GROUPS

Discuss these questions, then get a spokesperson to report your views to the rest of the class in a class discussion.

How much racism is there? Does it depend on the area in which you live? Do you think that society is more or less racist than it used to be?

Do you think the media encourages racism? Discuss the way that black people are portrayed by the media. Does the media present a stereotyped or distorted view of black/Asian people?

Is there more or less racial harassment than there used to be? What can be done to protect the victims of racial harassment? For example, in Leicester the council have installed emergency alarms in the homes of families felt to be at risk. Suggest other measures that the police, the local authority and the local community can take to protect people from racial attacks.

Do you think that, in time, racism will disappear altogether?

Discrimination and the law

The Race Relations Act, 1976 makes racial discrimination unlawful:

- in employment
- in education
- in the provision of goods and services, whether by individuals, businesses or local authorities
- in the sale, purchase and management of property.

The Act makes it an offence for a person or an institution, such as the local authority, to treat a person less favourably because of their race.

Proving discrimination

Proving discrimination is often not easy. But you do not have to prove that a person or institution actually stated that they intended to treat a particular group or individual less favourably on racial grounds. What you have to prove is that their actions led to discrimination. If you can prove that the effect of someone's actions was to lead to less favourable treatment, then it can be argued that discrimination has taken place.

The Commission for Racial Equality (CRE)

The Commission for Racial Equality is an organization set up to check that the Race Relations Act is working successfully and preventing discrimination.

The CRE can investigate the actions of local authorities and companies to see if the decisions taken and services provided resulted in discrimination because of race.

- During an investigation, the CRE will, if necessary, offer advice on how to make procedures fair and free from discrimination.
- In the rare cases where their advice is not accepted and acted upon, the CRE can start legal proceedings to force the company or local authority to change the way they operate.
- The CRE can also assist and advise individuals who wish to use the courts to protest against discrimination.

WHO CAN HELP?

The Commission for Racial Equality can be contacted at 10–12 Allington Street, London SW1E 5EH.

CASE 1

Messrs Khan, Iqbal, Iqbal and Javidi v Sunblest Bakeries Ltd

'Following a three-day hearing, Leeds Industrial Tribunal held that four black bakery workers were discriminated against at Hagenbachs factory in Wakefield. The discrimination occurred when Management at the Bakery failed to take steps to curb incidences of racial abuse, although they were aware of its existence.

'Messrs Anwar Khan, Zafar Iqbal, Javaid Iqbal (Pakistani) and Majid Javidi (Iranian) gave evidence that they regularly suffered racial abuse from other workers at the factory, which is owned by Sunblest Bakeries Ltd. The applicants also complained that they were deliberately over-looked during a round of promotions when they all appeared to be the obvious candidates for the higher posts available.

'The Bread Production Manager, who was responsible for selecting employees, for promotion, is alleged to have said, shortly before the promotions took place, that he would not have 'black bastards' running both shifts at the factory. The applicants raised this remark with the Bakery's Managing Director who said that he did not want to hear about it. He later denied that the matter had even been raised with him at all.

'The applicants also produced photographs of racist graffiti which appeared in the toilets and which they claimed supported their allegations about the level of abuse at the factory.'

CONSIDER

1 Do you think it is the employer's role to protect employees from racism in the workplace?

2 If it is, what should the employer do in such cases?

3 What effect do you think racist graffiti would have on black workers at the Bakery?

4 Do you think the fact that none of the black people were promoted is one of concern?

ROLE PLAY

In pairs, act out a scene in which someone who has been discriminated against by a restaurant/shop owner, landlady/landlord or employer describes the incident to a friend. Take it in turns to be the person who has been discriminated against, then join up with another pair and discuss what it felt like to be a victim of discrimination. Appoint someone to act as a spokesperson and report your views to the rest of the class in a class discussion.

FOR YOUR FILE

Do you think the Race Relations Act has been a success? Write a short statement giving reasons for your view.

Use the information on this page to prepare a fact-sheet for children aged 10/11 telling them about the Race Relations Act and explaining what the Commission for Racial Equality is.

CASE 2

Miss M J Williams v Chelsea Girl

Nineteen-year-old Marie Williams, a British-born black woman from Preston, saw a vacancy for a sales assistant advertised in the shop window of Chelsea Girl, Blackburn. On making an enquiry from the manageress of Chelsea Girl, Miss Williams was told to come back two days later as there had not been enough people applying for the job.

On her return two days later, she was again told by the manageress that not enough people had applied for the job. Three days after this Miss Williams again returned to Chelsea Girl only to be given the same message. Nearly one week later Miss Williams returned, and was told the manageress was too busy to see her and that the vacancy had been filled.

As the vacancy was still being displayed in Chelsea Girl's window at this time, Miss Williams felt upset and humiliated. She asked a passing white girl if she would go into Chelsea Girl and pretend she was interested in the vacancy. This girl was given an interview for the following Monday and this strengthened Miss Williams' suspicion that she had been treated less favourably because of her colour. This suspicion was further confirmed when the Job Centre later rang Chelsea Girl and established that interviews were to be held on the following Monday.

The Chelsea Girl's manageress told the Tribunal that she had decided not to employ Miss Williams because she lived some miles away in Preston. However, it was noted that some white applicants invited to interview also lived outside Blackburn, that Miss Williams was the only candidate within the specified age range of 18–23, and that the successful white applicant was 16 and lived as far from Blackburn as the applicant.

CONSIDER

1 Do you think that this whole incident resulted out of genuine misunderstanding?

2 If not, who do you think was at fault?

3 Why were they at fault?

4 What do you feel about the reasons the manageress gave for not employing Miss Williams?

5 How do you think employers can be prevented from discriminating against black applicants?

IN GROUPS

Carefully study the three cases described on this spread. All three give details of real incidents brought before the Civil Courts or industrial tribunals by the Commission for Racial Equality.

In your groups, discuss each case in turn. Then, appoint someone to act as spokesperson and report your views to the rest of the class in a class discussion.

CASE 3

Dr Singh

When Dr Singh visited a public house in Newcastle, he was refused entry because he was wearing a turban. Dr Singh subsequently complained to the Community Relations Council in Newcastle.

The owner of the public house denied unlawful discrimination against Dr Singh, but conceded that he operated a 'no hats' policy at the pub. He said that he wanted to avoid an 'imbalance' being created if a number of turban wearers collected together.

CONSIDER

1 The owner had a 'no hats' policy in his public house which applied to everybody coming there. How can this be seen as racially discriminating?

2 The owner said he was concerned about a number of turban wearers collecting together. Would he feel the same way about a number of tweed jacket wearers collecting together?

3 Can you think of other instances where people or organizations apply rules which supposedly apply to everybody, but really their effect is felt mostly by black people?

4 Do you think that people like the owner should be allowed to decide who is and is not allowed into the public house or other place?

Young can overcome prejudice says study

By LIZ LIGHTFOOT and JOHN QUINN

YOUNG blacks are forging ahead to create a new middle class in Britain.

They are reaching the top in their professions and starting new businesses – despite racism and discrimination.

The first national survey of the more than a million Afro-Caribbeans in Britain shows that there are thousands of self-made businessmen and women, lawyers, accountants and managers.

Although half of the black population earns less than £15,000, this new survey – the most comprehensive analysis ever undertaken – shows a large middle band of one in three earning between £15,000 and £30,000.

One in ten owns stocks and shares, more than half have bank savings and 50 per cent save with a building society.

Schooling

Television images of riot-torn Broadwater Farm estate are not representative of most black homes where families have comfortable, if not often luxurious, lifestyles.

Education is seen as the way forward for eight in ten, who regard it as very important. Young black people are more likely than their parents to continue full-time study after the school leaving age.

But despite their optimism, most black people complain of daily racism and discrimination.

The *Mail on Sunday* (10/2/91)

	Yes	No	Don't Know
Have whites now accepted people of your racial background as part of British society?	22	60	18
Should people of your racial background try to preserve as much of your culture and own way of life as possible?	80	4	16
Can people of your racial background rely on the police to protect them from racist violence?	11	75	14
Would you ever think of marrying someone not of your racial background?	33	43	24
Do you agree that white people should not adopt black children?	43	33	22
Is it difficult for someone of your racial background to secure a good job?	54	27	19

Results of a survey of 896 black people in 1990–91

IN GROUPS

Discuss the results of the survey (above). Do its findings surprise you?

Do you think it is important in a multi-cultural society for people from different social, cultural and ethnic backgrounds to preserve their own cultures and ways of life? Give the reasons for your views.

What are your views on 'mixed-race' relationships? Why do you think 43 per cent of black people said they would never contemplate marrying someone from a different racial background? Do you think a survey of white people's opinions would produce similar results?

Do you agree that white people should not be allowed to adopt black children? Make a list of the arguments for and against allowing white families to adopt black/Asian children.

Why do you think so many black/Asian people do not feel they can rely on the police to protect them? What further steps do you think the police should take to protect black/Asian people? How can the police win back the confidence of black communities?

FOR YOUR FILE

'The trouble is that surveys like this (see *Mail on Sunday* article) only get reported once in a while. Most stories in the media are about black people getting into trouble or about racism. The media are to blame for perpetuating myths and stereotypes about black people.' Do you agree? Write a short article expressing your views.

Cultural Crossroads

'I am British, but I'm also Asian. It's a matter of having the space to express them both'

My 12-year-old brother wears his England colours tracksuit like a second skin, but white children often jeer at his choice of team. His first skin is black, and, as he should know, there's still no black in this country's Union Jack.

He'll be reminded of this in child's play and every day of his life. Both my brother and I are second generation Asians living in a multi-coloured, multi-cultured society that still hasn't learned a thing about the potential to be gained from cross-culture, exemplified by this young Asian cheering England FC.

Like many other young British Asians, I parade an identity that has been cultivated, carved and at times distorted by the hands of a culture that is, for me, both Asian and British. The effect of one culture slapped on to another, contrary, culture creates something that's beautifully complete, but somehow open and uneven where the elements of two different cultures have just failed to blend.

This is my own self-definition, for I disagree with those blacks and whites who seek to find only cracks of confusion and isolation in my cultural make-up. Growing up across two cultures may have its difficulties, but they are only made into problems by the closed minds of others.

Talking to white friends makes me realize that my consciousness of my identity is more tangible than theirs because, throughout my life, I've been forced primarily by others, to grapple with questions about my identity.

As a child, the discovery and subsequent assertion that I was different was distressing, particularly when, instead of finding respect for that difference, I met only ignorance, ridicule and exclusion. I remember my fraught attempts to assimilate into the dominant white culture around me. This meant abbreviating my Vedic name, Apala, to the English-sounding, English-approved Paula, up until I left grammar school.

This early self-denial of my Asian-ness still cuts me up and I recoil with shame at feeling the need to conform in such a soul-selling way. But the real fault lies in a society that generates a low self-opinion among blacks, forcing many of us to undermine our respective traditions. I recognize that familiar behaviour in my brother – 'Sam, not Shimon' – who'll stress quite adamantly that, first and foremost, he's British.

I am British, but I'm also Asian. It's not a matter of forsaking one culture for the other, but having the space to express them both, individually or together. The worst consequence is encountering ignorance and racism as part of that experience. But this isn't an inherent weakness to being raised between two cultures, rather it's a weakness in those who judge me. To be raised as an Asian-Briton, enables me to pick and mix those qualities that I like best from the two cultures that I claim, to create the vibrant cultural fabric that is my identity.

Marxism Today (Oct 1989)

Tanuja's Story

Tanuja Shah could never imagine living anywhere except England.
'My family arrived here from West Africa when I was four years old, so I've done all my growing up in this country. This is home for me.'

Currently doing a business and finance course at college, Tanuja finds it easy to combine the Indian lifestyle, upheld by her parents at home, with the ordinary social activities enjoyed by her friends at college.

'Of course I have restrictions and commitments to my family that my English friends do not have,' admits Tanuja. 'Although my family aren't particularly religious, we do uphold the traditions of the Oshwal community, and that means going to the temple at festival times, and behaving in a way that's socially acceptable, as set down in the laws of the religion.' (There are approximately 15,000 people nationwide in the Oshwal community and they're all followers of the Jain religion.)

'My family have chosen to take the name of the community which is Shah – we use that as a surname. I think that other Indian families adopt the name of their communities, which is why there are so many people called Patel.'

Although Tanuja is almost 18, she still listens closely to her parents' advice, follows their wishes, and would never do anything that might upset them.

'My brother is five years older than me and he still lives at home,' she says. 'Because he's a boy he has a lot more independence, whereas I have certain duties as a daughter, such as cooking and helping my mother. On the whole, we're a very close unit. I think that's one of the big differences between English and Indian families, as many of my English friends hardly see their relatives. I see my cousins all the time and my parents prefer it if I go out with them because they know I'm safe. My English friends are very understanding about this: they're interested to know as much as they can about my background and they never make fun of me. When I go out with them I don't drink alcohol or smoke because it's forbidden. I've never been tempted to try it and I want to bring up my children in the same way.'

Just Seventeen

Building my own island

No-one's tried to build a bridge
Across three thousand miles
And two cultures before,
People keep expecting me to.
I've decided to ignore them all,
And I'm building my own
Island somewhere in the middle
In easy reach of both sides.

Hummarah Quddoos

IN PAIRS

What do you learn from Tanuja and Apala about what it is like to be a teenager from an ethnic minority growing up in Britain today? Do you think their experiences are typical?

Hummarah Quddoos says she is 'building my own island somewhere in the middle'. What do you think she means? How does this compare with what Tanuja and Apala say?

HOMOSEXUALITY

A homosexual is a person who is attracted to and may fall in love with someone of the same sex – in the same way as a heterosexual is attracted to and may fall in love with someone of the opposite sex. Homosexual relationships are just as loving and real as heterosexual relationships.

Apart from open prejudice, homosexuals have to cope with a society geared towards heterosexuality and laws that discriminate against them.

Attitudes towards homosexuality

'Preconditioned by things such as TV and advertising it's assumed that every boy and girl is 'straight' [heterosexual] . . . There is tremendous pressure on us all to conform; to become objects of desire to the opposite sex, to get married and to have children. . . . The problem is intensified by the fact that in our culture there is still a taboo against homosexuality. This taboo exists mainly because there is an old idea that 'sex equals reproduction' and, as loving someone of the same sex can't produce babies, many see it as 'unnatural', 'abnormal', even 'perverted'.

Insulting words such as 'poofter', 'faggot', 'queer', 'bender' and 'dyke' have been invented to reinforce this prejudice and they cause a lot of harm. These prejudices make many gay [homosexual] people feel that if they are attracted to the same sex there must be something wrong with them and they end up feeling bad about themselves and their sexuality.'
Homosexuality, Rosalyn Chissick

'We must try to see homosexuality not as a sin or a sickness, but more as a handicap.'
Dr Robert Runcie, former Archbishop of Canterbury

'In sacred scripture they [homosexuals] are condemned. . . . This does not permit us to conclude that all those who suffer from homosexuality are personally responsible for it, but it does point to the fact that homosexual acts are disordered and can in no case be approved of.'
Declaration of Sexual Ethics, 1975 (Roman Catholic)

'For homosexual men and women, permanent relationships characterized by love can be an appropriate and Christian way of expressing their sexuality.'
Methodist report

'We believe that fear or hatred of homosexuals is a social evil, similar to anti-semitism, racism, slavery, and with

Gay rights rally, London 1991

the same evil consequences. It harms both the victimized individuals, and the society which tolerates it.'
Towards a Charter of Homosexual Rights

Homosexuals and AIDS

AIDS has made a lot of people prejudiced against homosexuals, because so far in Great Britain AIDS has affected more male homosexuals that heterosexuals. Gay men have had a reputation for being promiscuous, so some people have blamed them for the spread of the HIV virus. In reality, the sexual habits of gay people are as varied as those of heterosexuals. Some have several partners, others stick to one partner. In fact, since the threat of AIDS became apparent, gay men have adopted the policy of safe sex more readily than heterosexuals.

Homosexuality and the law

Almost every European country has, at some point in its history, banned homosexuality. Today, the overwhelming majority of European countries have at least partially legalized same-sex relationships.

The UK has more laws which explicitly, or in practice, discriminate against homosexuals than any other European country.

Sally's story

SALLY, 22, BOOKSHOP WORKER.

"I can cope with being a lesbian now because I'm older. I've learned from my mistakes, and from the things I've suffered. Also, I finally got lucky – I met women of my own age who had been through the same experiences as me, so I found people to talk to at last.

"All I remember about being a teenager is being scared all the time. There wasn't anyone I could talk to about how I felt, and I was just terrified.

"Like, if it got out that I thought I was a lesbian, how would my life be changed? Would people shout at me in the street? Would my dad chuck me out of the house? Was it against the law to be a lesbian? I just didn't have any answers.

"And now that I've got lesbian friends to talk to, they say it was very much the same when they were younger, too. Which is a shame, I think."

Mark's story

MARK, 17, UNEMPLOYED.

"I've always been relaxed about my sexual identity. I know gays who say their life as a teenager was just hell, they had a really bad time, but it never happened to me.

"The only thing that ever worried me was how my mates would react. I mean, I didn't just blurt it out one night – 'Hi, lads, I'll have a pint of lager and by the way, did I mention that I'm having an affair with another boy?' – but I didn't want to hide it, either.

"In the end I just told them, and said if they didn't like it then I was better off without them. But most of them were great. I needn't have worried."

Mizz (Issue 56)

MYTHS ABOUT HOMOSEXUALITY

1 You can tell by looking at someone whether they are homosexual
Many people think that all lesbians (homosexual women) are butch and all gay men are effeminate. However, homosexuals are as varied in their physical appearance and dress as heterosexuals.

2 Women who are not attractive to men become lesbians
This is not true. Women are *not* lesbians because they have been rejected by men, but because they are only attracted to women.

3 Homosexuals dislike people of the opposite sex
Lesbians are often thought of as man-haters. Gay men are often portrayed as being afraid of women. In fact, homosexuals often have strong friendships with people of the opposite sex. It's just that they are not sexually attracted to them.

4 Homosexuals fancy everybody who is of the same sex as them
Some people believe that homosexuals will 'try it on' with every same-sex person they meet. This myth has come about through lack of knowledge about homosexuals. This ignorance has led to unnecessary fear. Homosexuals are just as selective about who they fancy as heterosexuals.

5 Homosexuals want to change their sex
People who want to change their sex are called transsexuals. They believe themselves to be trapped in the wrong body. Homosexuals are happy with their sex and have no desire to change it.

Homosexuality: different laws across Europe

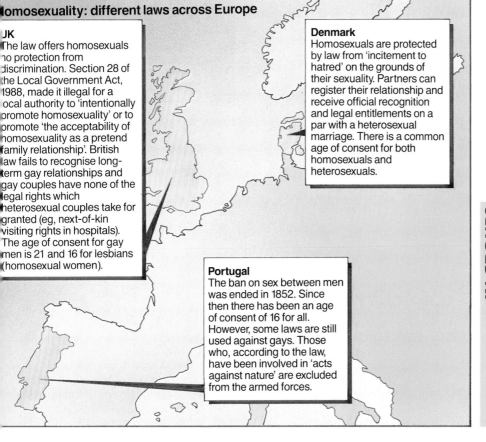

UK
The law offers homosexuals no protection from discrimination. Section 28 of the Local Government Act, 1988, made it illegal for a local authority to 'intentionally promote homosexuality' or to promote 'the acceptability of homosexuality as a pretend family relationship'. British law fails to recognise long-term gay relationships and gay couples have none of the legal rights which heterosexual couples take for granted (eg, next-of-kin visiting rights in hospitals). The age of consent for gay men is 21 and 16 for lesbians (homosexual women).

Denmark
Homosexuals are protected by law from 'incitement to hatred' on the grounds of their sexuality. Partners can register their relationship and receive official recognition and legal entitlements on a par with a heterosexual marriage. There is a common age of consent for both homosexuals and heterosexuals.

Portugal
The ban on sex between men was ended in 1852. Since then there has been an age of consent of 16 for all. However, some laws are still used against gays. Those who, according to the law, have been involved in 'acts against nature' are excluded from the armed forces.

IN GROUPS

1 Discuss the statements made in the section 'Attitudes towards homosexuality'. Say which, if any, you agree with and why. Then, report the different views of the members of your group in a class discussion.

2 Discuss the different laws about homosexuality that exist in EC countries. Do you think Britain's laws on homosexuality should be changed in any way? As the EC moves towards closer political union, do you think it should introduce common policies on homosexual rights?

What makes you angry?

'Someone criticizing my appearance.'

'Being treated as if I'm a child.'

'Double standards. Adults who tell you not to do something, then do it themselves.'

'Being patronized.'

'People talking about me as if I'm not there.'

'When someone won't listen to what I've got to say.'

'People who say unkind things about you behind your back.'

'Being let down by someone you thought you could rely on.'

What triggers anger?

Dr Kevin Howells, a Birmingham university psychologist, suggests that there are four broad categories of trigger factors – the things that make people angry:

1 **Classic frustration:** being prevented from achieving a particular goal. Example: You are picked to play for a team, but unable to do so because you have to attend a family gathering.

2 **Thwarted expectation:** looking forward to an event, then being disappointed. Example: You had been looking forward to going out, then your friend rings at the last minute to say they can't go.

3 **Violated rules:** We each have our own set of rules/codes of conduct we expect others to follow and we get angry when people break them. Examples: Someone lies to you or someone barges in front of you in a queue.

4 **Threats to self-esteem:** a person does or says something that threatens to show you or up or make you lose face. Example: Someone 'takes the mickey' out of something you say in front of other people.

Expressing 'righteous anger'.

IN PAIRS

What kinds of behaviour make you angry? Think about situations involving your parents, your brothers and sisters, your friends, your teachers, other adults. List the things that trigger your anger in four columns, according to which category of trigger factor you think that they belong to. Are there some things which don't fit into any of the four columns?

FOR YOUR FILE

Write a letter to a newspaper expressing your views on an issue that you feel very strongly about.

IN GROUPS

'Righteous anger'

As well as getting angry about behaviour that affects us personally, we also get angry about human behaviour that we personally consider to be morally unacceptable – for example, torture, sexual abuse, prejudice and discrimination, cruelty to animals, biological and chemical weapons. Discuss the issues that make you feel 'righteous anger'. Which issue(s) do you feel most strongly about? Do you express your anger in any way? Talk about people who express their anger by joining pressure groups, mounting campaigns and organizing protests. What do you think is the best way to draw attention to an issue and to get something done about it?

Channelling your anger

There is nothing unhealthy about feeling angry. It's a normal emotion, like joy or disappointment. What matters is how you handle your anger.

How do you behave when you are angry? Do you try to state your viewpoint calmly and logically? Do you storm into a rage and start shouting and slamming about? Or do you say nothing, bottling up your anger so that it seethes inside you?

Many people are inhibited about showing their anger. However much they are provoked, they never react angrily. Responding passively, when deep down inside you are fuming, is a bad idea. It's bad for your health and it doesn't solve anything. If you don't show people that their behaviour is upsetting you, then the chances are they'll continue to go on upsetting you – either because they don't realize you're angry, or because they think they can get away with it.

Responding aggressively is also a bad idea. 'If you attack someone verbally or physically,' says Professor Cary Cooper of the University of Manchester Institute of Science and Technology, 'they are likely to want to defend themselves. They certainly won't be in any mood to listen reasonably to your grievances.'

How to handle your anger

According to Anne Dickson, the assertive management of anger involves learning to communicate your feelings and to release your anger.
To communicate effectively, you first need to work out exactly what is making you so angry. Once you have analysed why you are angry, the next step is to get your message across. Your aim, says Professor Cooper, must be to express your anger in a constructive way. 'You should try to get your feelings across in a way that doesn't physically affect the person or cause them to become defensive.' Throwing things or hurling insults may get the anger out of your system, but it's much more effective if you can manage not to lose your temper or only lose it as a last resort.

It is important to release your anger, rather than to bottle it up. But what happens if the consequences of expressing your anger might be to cause a family feud or to get you suspended from school? Even in such circumstances, Professor Cooper maintains that you should be able to communicate your feelings, provided that you control your anger in the right way.

But if you don't feel you can confront the person who is making you angry, you can always use the 'empty chair' technique. Shut yourself in your room and imagine that the person you want to talk to is sitting in a chair. Then, say all the things that you'd want to say to them if they really were sitting there. Alternatively, write down your feelings in a letter or your diary, making sure that you either destroy what you've written or that you keep it somewhere where no one else will find it.

And find a physical way of releasing the stress in your body. 'Angry feelings,' says Anne Dickson, 'won't be released by a few choked tears; release needs large, vigorous movements.' Go out for a run, or a swim. If that's not possible, shut yourself in your room and punch the pillows.

When I'm angry

LOIS: 'I go up to my room and put my headphones on and listen to music and refuse to talk to anyone. I bottle it up, I suppose.'

JEFF: 'I've got a foul temper. I shout and stomp about, slamming doors. It gets it out of my system and it clears the air.'

NADINE: 'I try to be assertive and avoid losing my cool. If necessary, I count to ten before saying anything, so I don't say things I might regret later. If I'm really furious, I may walk away. It gives you time to work out what's making you angry and to plan what you're going to say.'

ASHLEY: 'I find it helps if I do something physical – like go for a swim or a bike ride. It helps to get it out of my system, but only if I then work out a way of communicating my anger.'

JIM: 'I don't see the point of getting all steamed up. In my experience, it doesn't work. I just get moody and go quiet. It's my way of coping and it doesn't do anyone any harm.'

IN PAIRS

Discuss the way these five teenagers handle their anger. Which of them handle their anger well? Which of them handle it badly?

Study the article, 'How to handle your anger'. Why is it important to learn to express your anger? What is the best way to handle your anger?

Draw up a list of 'Do's' and 'Don'ts' giving practical advice to teenagers on how to handle their anger.

FOR YOUR FILE

Either write a story about a person expressing their anger or write about a time when you felt very angry. Explain what triggered your anger. Say whether you think you handled your anger constructively and whether or not you could have handled it in a more effective way.

Feeling anxious

Anxiety is a normal, healthy emotion which everyone experiences. Psychologist Dorothy Rowe refers to it as a type of 'growing pain'.

As you grow up, lots of things start changing and it can be difficult to know how to cope. Your relationship with your parents alters as you begin to take responsibility for your own decisions. You may have a girlfriend or boyfriend for the first time. There are exams to prepare for and your future to think about.

Feeling anxious keeps you on your toes, heightens your senses and can improve your performance. If you didn't feel some anxiety about getting good grades, then you probably wouldn't work as hard as you need to in order to get them.

But anxiety can get out of hand. The pressures of getting all your work done and coping with new responsibilities and new relationships can lead to deep feelings of fear and insecurity. When this happens, you can start suffering from stress which can make you ill and seriously affect your performance.

What is stress?

According to Dr John Bonn, former director of the stress management unit at St Bartholemew's Hospital, London, 'Stress has to do with feeling unable to cope with what's expected of you. People who consistently doubt they can cope will experience chronic anxiety.' People may experience stress because the pressures of everyday life mount up and they become over-anxious. Stress may also be triggered by external events over which a person has no direct control, such as a death or a change in family circumstances.

Worrying shows on the outside.

How does worrying affect you?

Worrying doesn't just make you feel depressed, it actually affects you physically, too. If you're feeling under pressure, you'll probably also be feeling . . .

- TIRED. Having a problem that's always on your mind makes it difficult for you to sleep – and if you do sleep, it'll probably be interrupted and by the time you get up, you'll be grumpy and exhausted. Not the best start to the day!

- TENSE. Letting a problem build-up inside you leaves you feeling irritable and on edge – and less able to deal with other niggly worries.

- RUN-DOWN. Worrying all the time puts a strain on your immune system. So you're more likely to pick-up colds and other viral infections. And if you do catch a cold, you're less able to fight it off so it'll linger around for ages.

- Feeling worried means you'll be more likely to suffer headaches and feel bored, restless and short-tempered.

- Worrying doesn't just affect you inside – it shows up on the outside too. As well as feeling generally run down, your skin and hair may look unhealthy – and you could even develop a stress-related skin problem.

Jackie (23/3/91)

IN GROUPS

Below is a list of some of the possible causes of stress among teenagers. On your own at first, study the list and rank each reason on a scale from 1 – 16 (1 = not important, 16 = extremely important). When you have finished, add any other causes of stress you can think of to the list and rank them. Then, share your views in a group discussion.

Breaking up with boyfriend/girlfriend
Preparing for exams
Death of a parent, sister or brother
Pressure to follow group's code of behaviour
Moving area and changing school
Concerns about their own sexuality
Pressure to conform to parents' religious beliefs
Conflicts with brothers and sisters
Having no close friends
Parents' divorce or separation
Getting into trouble with the law
Choosing a career
Concerns about their own appearance
Getting teased/bullied
Parents being very strict
Death of a friend

Coping with stress

Coping with stress involves taking steps to stop it from developing or managing stress once it has arisen. The techniques below are useful ways of avoiding stress and dealing with stress.

---

1 GET ORGANIZED

- Make lists
- Set priorities
- Plan the use of your time
- Complete one task before starting another.

'A lot of stress among teenagers could be avoided by better time management.' (Head of Year 10)

---

2 THINK POSITIVE

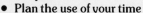
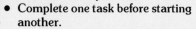

- Plan a way of changing things and put it into action
- Keep things in perspective
- Have something to look forward to
- Recognize things you achieve and reward yourself in some way.

'Constructive thinking is very important. It helps you to identify your problems. List the options open to you, work out the pros and cons, and see where you can make changes to relieve stress.' (Professor Cary Cooper)

---

3 LEARN TO RELAX

- Allow yourself time to relax after a stressful period
- Take regular exercise
- Eat a balanced diet
- Learn relaxation techniques.

When you are under stress, the body produces a number of different hormones, including adrenaline. Regular exercise, such as swimming or dancing is the best method of discharging the biochemical effects of stress from your body.

---

4 STAY IN CONTROL

- Set yourself reachable targets
- Have realistic expectations
- Be assertive
- Take responsibility for what you do and think.

'It's no good expecting things to change unless you are prepared to be assertive and express your feelings. And it's no good blaming external circumstances, when you fail to do things. Managing stress involves accepting responsibility and taking charge of your own life.' (Adele Stewart, Counsellor)

---

5 TALK IT OVER

- Find someone to talk to
- Identify the real cause of your stress
- Ask for advice
- Make up your own mind what to do.

'Whatever you do, don't bottle things up. That will only make you feel worse. Find a person you can trust and tell them what's worrying you and how you feel.' (Doctor)

ROLE PLAY

In groups, study the information on these pages and note down any important points that are made. Then, role play a radio phone-in programme in which a counsellor offers teenagers who phone in advice on how to cope with stress. Refer to your notes if necessary.

IN GROUPS

Decide who it would be best to talk to if you were suffering from stress caused by (**a**) school-work, (**b**) worries about your sexuality, (**c**) problems with parents, (**d**) problems with friends, (**e**) anxiety about the future.

'I talk to my older sister, because I know she will listen and take me seriously.' (Robert, 15)

'I talk to my mum, because she really understands.' (Marcia, 14)

'I have found it is better to go to a friend than an adult. A kid you're close to is in the same boat as you and will usually understand.' (Denise, 17)

'I don't talk about my problems to anyone. Why? Because people have always used and abused my feelings.' (Ginny, 15)

'Writing everything down is more helpful to me than talking. It really puts everything in perspective.' (Royston, 16)

'When I was under stress, I talked to a counsellor. She accepted what I said and didn't try to minimize my feelings.' (Raoul, 15)

WHO CAN HELP?

For advice on counselling services in your area, write to The National Association of Young People's Counselling and Advisory Services (NAYPCAS), 17–23 Albion Street, Leicester LE1 6GD.

WHAT ARE THE CAUSES OF UNEMPLOYMENT?

An unemployed person is someone who is seeking a job but is unable to find work. Whether or not a person will be unemployed during their working lifetime depends on a number of factors, such as the type of career they choose, where they live, how industries change and develop and what happens to the country's economy.

TYPES OF UNEMPLOYMENT

There are several different types of unemployment.

TRANSITIONAL UNEMPLOYMENT

Workers who do certain jobs often have short periods of unemployment between finishing one job and starting another. For example, a designer may finish one contract and be forced to have a few weeks' break while she looks for another job to start. Transitional unemployment is short-term and is always present in any economy.

SEASONAL UNEMPLOYMENT

Certain jobs are seasonal, so there is more demand for workers at particular times of the year. For example, more agricultural workers are needed at harvest time, and the tourist and building industries employ more people in the summer than in the winter months.

STRUCTURAL UNEMPLOYMENT

The demand for goods and services is constantly changing. As a result, some industries contract and need fewer workers, while others may expand and need more workers. Structural unemployment occurs when firms close down and there are not enough jobs in expanding industries for all those made redundant. Even when there are new jobs, they may not be suitable, or require different skills. For example, a factory may close with the loss of several hundred jobs, at the same time as a new shopping complex is being opened. It is unlikely that all those employed at the factory will find work in the shopping complex.

Similarly, new jobs are not always available in the area where the job losses occur. If workers are to find new jobs, they may have to consider moving areas and this may not be possible for either personal or financial reasons. This means that levels of unemployment often vary from one region to another.

TECHNOLOGICAL UNEMPLOYMENT

Developments in new technology have led to increases in unemployment, as jobs that were once done by hand are now done by computer. For example, fewer workers are now needed on factory production lines, since many jobs are now performed by robots.

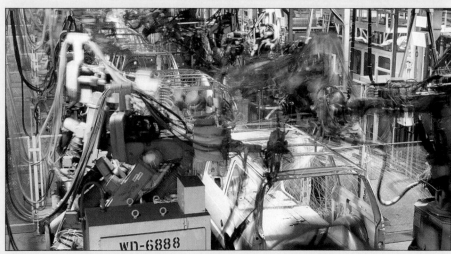

IN PAIRS

Study the information on these pages and decide in which category of unemployment these people belong:

(a) A labourer on a building site who is laid-off because of bad weather during January and February.

(b) An office worker who is made redundant because a recession means that the company has few orders and is cutting back staff.

(c) A factory worker who is made redundant because the company has installed new machinery and their job has 'disappeared'.

(d) A worker in a toy factory who loses their job in an area of high unemployment because the company has decided to invest in building a new factory in another part of the country.

(e) A person with very restricted mobility who simply cannot find a suitable job.

(f) A roofer who is temporarily out of work for a few weeks between jobs.

(g) A person who has no full-time job and is currently on a government training scheme.

Unemployment in your area

Investigate unemployment in your area during the past ten years. What is the current level of unemployment? How has the level of unemployment risen/fallen in your area compared with the national average over the past ten years? What factors have influenced the level of unemployment in your area? Report your findings to the rest of the class.

Unemployment and ethnic origin

'Unemployment varies according to ethnic origin. Government figures for 1989 put the white unemployment rate at 7 per cent. Other groups were as follows: Pakistani/ Bangladeshi 21.8%; West Indian/ Guyanese 14.4%; Indian 9.4%; all other groups 7.9%.'

The *Guardian* (26/2/91)

What do you think (a) the government, (b) employers should do to ensure that people from ethnic minorities do not have higher unemployment levels?

FOR YOUR FILE

Make a glossary of the key terms that are introduced on this page.

The 'hidden unemployed'

In Britain, the unemployment figures are measured by counting those people who are eligible for, and claiming unemployment benefit. However, many people think that the unemployment figures are misleading, not only due to the way the statistics are calculated, but because of the number of people who simply do not appear on the figures.

Unemployment figures do not include, for example – 16 or 17 year olds who have not found a YT placement, students who are unemployed during the holidays and women who paid a reduced rate of National Insurance when they were working. None of these groups are eligible to claim benefit and are, therefore, not registered as unemployed. Unemployment figures also ignore the number of people who are unemployed, but claim some other type of benefit – for example – people claiming disability allowances, carers and single parents.

People like this are sometimes called the 'hidden unemployed'. It has been estimated that if these people were included in the unemployment statistics it would add at least 1 million people to the figures.

CYCLICAL UNEMPLOYMENT

This type of unemployment affects the whole country and occurs when there is a general decline in the demand for goods and services. A period during which there are low levels of demand is known as a recession and a long and severe recession is called a slump. During a recession, there are high levels of unemployment as industries and businesses close down and cut levels of production because they are unable to sell their goods and services.

With more people out of work, there is less demand for goods and services, and more businesses close down. The process of recession is therefore a vicious circle. The recession can only really end when demand starts to rise again. Industries and businesses can then start to grow and unemployment will fall as new jobs are created. With more people in work demand will grow, and so on. Economists, however, are divided about how to help the country out of a recession. Some believe that after a time a recession cures itself, because workers become willing to accept lower pay, shops lower the price of goods in order to sell them and the demand for goods starts to grow again. Others argue that cutting wages only leads to a further fall in demand and makes the recession worse. They say the way out of a recession is for the government to spend money in order to stimulate demand and to make the economy start growing again.

RESIDUAL UNEMPLOYMENT

Even when the economy is booming there will always be some people who are unemployed. There are people with mental or physical disabilities for whom there are no suitable jobs. And there are those who choose not to join in 'normal' society, and don't have jobs.

◄ *New technology means that fewer workers are needed.*

WHAT ARE THE EFFECTS OF UNEMPLOYMENT?

THE ECONOMIC COST

When people are unemployed, there is a waste of resources. Unemployed people are unable to contribute to the economy by providing goods and services.

The more people there are unemployed, the more it costs the government in benefit payments and lost revenue from taxes.

A SOCIAL COST?

Some people blame the rise in unemployment for the increase in crimes and the urban riots that occurred in the 1980s and early 1990s. They argue that boredom and frustration among young people led to more street crime and more drug abuse. However, it is difficult to prove whether there is a connection between unemployment and crime. Others argue that unemployment is just one of a number of factors that led to more crime.

'Unemployment remains nevertheless an evil that touches all the community. There can be no doubt that it was a major factor in the complex pattern of conditions which lies at the root of the disorders in Brixton and elsewhere. In a materialistic society, the relative (not by any means – given our social security system – absolute) deprivation it entails is keenly felt, and idleness gives time for resentment and envy to grow.'

The Scarman Report: The Brixton Disorders,
Lord Scarman

The most obvious economic cost is the bill for unemployment benefit.

During the financial year which ran from April 1989 to April 1990 the cost to the taxpayer of benefits to the unemployed was £4,740 million, or £2,946 per unemployed person. But this was only one part of the cost to the Government.

If claimants had been working, it is estimated that they would have paid £3,436 million in income tax. Both employees and employers also have to pay National Insurance contributions and if the unemployed had been working this would have raised a further £2,800 million.

Unemployed people tend to spend less in the shops on goods such as furniture and clothes, which are subject to Value Added Tax (VAT), and alcohol, cigarettes and tobacco, which are subject to excise duties. The cost of these losses to the Government is put at around £2,000 million a year.

Add in administration costs and the total cost of unemployment in 1989-90 comes out at £13,374 million, or £8,296 per unemployed person.

The Education Guardian (26/2/91)

THE HUMAN COST

Studies of how unemployment affects people suggest that unemployed people are more likely to be anxious and depressed. In his book *The Unemployment Handbook*, Guy Dauncey suggests that a job, regular training or education gives a person support in five basic ways:

1 A job gives you a sense of purpose and direction.
2 A job provides regular daily activity.
3 Your job gives you a sense of identity and self-respect.
4 A job provides companionship and friendship.
5 A job provides money.

If these supports are taken away, a person can easily become depressed.

WHAT IS IT LIKE BEING UNEMPLOYED?

Four young people Fatima Meah, Abigail Macnamara, Denise Cunningham and Jackie Jeeves talk about what it feels like to be unemployed.

Passing the time

– Besides looking for jobs, you read comics, watch television, play records, go looking in shop windows. You can't afford the bus fares to visit your mates if they live out of walking distance. You make yourself useful doing the housework. At first, I used to keep the house absolutely clean and tidy, for something to do.

– You do anything to occupy your mind. Sometimes my mum gives me money for doing the housework. I have to cook my brother's meals, and if I've been out on a course or something, he has a go at me when it's not ready.

– I just go to my mum, and now I owe her a lot of money. But if my mum was unemployed I'd be completely stuck.

Your family and friends

– People ask what you do and you say nothing and they say never mind and that's the end of the subject – nothing more to talk about. You might lie because you're embarrassed about it to try to cover up, and make excuses if they ask more.

– They look down on you as if you're a layabout, especially if they're working. You feel you're the only one because all your friends seem to have jobs. You get very lonely, and you have no topic of conversation. My boyfriend says, 'Why don't you get a job, at least you'd have something to talk about.'

– At home it's really depressing. You tend to get moody and unsociable. You lose confidence in yourself so that when you do get an interview you don't expect to get the job.

Adapted from *Girls Are Powerful*, ed. Susan Hemmings

Coping with unemployment

If you are unemployed, the most important thing is to adopt a positive attitude. For a start, don't stop looking for work. Is there a centre for the unemployed or job club that you could go to? Find out if there are any training opportunities available or classes that you can attend. Make use of your skills and interests. Is there any voluntary work that you could do? Set yourself a series of targets and organize how best to spend your time so that you don't get into the habit of just drifting from day to day.

Coping With Unemployment,
Stuart Lewis

A Job Centre

What do you think are the social effects of unemployment? Do you think unemployment is a key factor in causing higher levels of crime, especially street crime and drug-taking? Discuss what Fatima, Abigail, Denise and Jackie say about being unemployed. How does unemployment affect their lives? What effect do you think being made redundant would have on the lives of the following people: (**a**) a person in their twenties who has just got married, (**b**) a single parent with a baby, (**c**) a married person, with a partner who works part-time, and two teenage children, (**d**) a single person in their early fifties?

How could life for the unemployed be improved? Should there be more concessions for unemployed people, e.g. reduced fares on public transport? Consider the cost of any suggestions you make. Who would fund your proposals?

In pairs, act out a scene in which a reporter interviews an unemployed person about how unemployment has affected their life and how they spend their time. Before you begin the role play work out what questions the interviewer will ask and how the unemployed person will reply.

Discuss the advice Stuart Lewis gives on how to cope with unemployment.

Discuss how you think you would feel if you were unemployed for a long time. How well do you think you would be able to cope? Think about each other's skills and interests. Suggest ways that you might use your time positively if you were ever unemployed.

FOR YOUR FILE

Either interview a person who is unemployed and write about their life or write a story or poem about an unemployed person, describing their thoughts and feelings.

AN ENERGY CRISIS?

Effect of 'acid rain' on trees.

Our lifestyle depends on energy. We use energy for cooking and heating and powering electrical equipment in our homes, our schools, our hospitals, our factories, our offices and our shops. We also use energy for our transport.

Problems with fossil fuels

In Britain, over 90 per cent of our energy is produced by burning fossil fuels, such as coal, oil and natural gas. The first problem with fossil fuels is that they pollute the atmosphere. When fossil fuels are burned, they produce carbon dioxide, one of the gases which contributes to the 'greenhouse effect'. Burning fossil fuels also produces millions of tonnes of sulphur dioxide and nitrogen oxides each year. These are the gases which react in the atmosphere to produce 'acid rain'. This causes serious damage to lakes and rivers, forests and buildings.

Another problem with fossil fuels is that they are finite resources. Once they have been burned, they cannot be used again and, in due course, supplies will run out. There are still plentiful reserves of coal in Britain, but the rate at which oil is being consumed means that the world's oil reserves will probably run out sometime around 2050. Supplies of natural gas will probably run out at about the same time.

An inefficient process

When fossil fuels are burned, a lot of energy is usually lost in the form of heat. The diagram shows how, in a coal-burning power station, only about 35 per cent of the energy produced from the coal is actually turned into electricity.

What is the greenhouse effect?

The 'greenhouse effect' is the gradual raising of the temperature of the air in the lower atmosphere, as the result of the accumulation of gases such as carbon dioxide, methane, nitrous oxide, chloroflurocarbons and ozone. These gases occur naturally in the atmosphere and act like a pane of glass in a greenhouse – letting in the sunshine, but keeping the long-wave out-going energy in the atmosphere. By this process the temperature of the Earth **should** remain stable. However, as the result of the burning of fossil fuels, the amount of carbon dioxide in the atmosphere has increased drastically (26 per cent between 1860 and 1986), altering the heat balance of the lower atmosphere and 'warming up' the Earth. This warming up could have serious consequences. It would only take a rise of 5 °C in the average temperature of the Earth to melt the polar ice caps (causing widescale flooding) and a disruption of the ocean currents and climate.

An energy policy for the next century

In developing an energy policy for the next century we need to look at ways of meeting our energy needs that are economic, efficient and will not damage the environment. This unit looks at the present situation and explores the main alternatives:

1 Promoting energy conservation, improving the efficiency and lessening the environmental damage caused by present methods of energy production.

2 Increasing the number of nuclear power stations.

3 Developing renewable energy resources, such as wind power, water power and solar power.

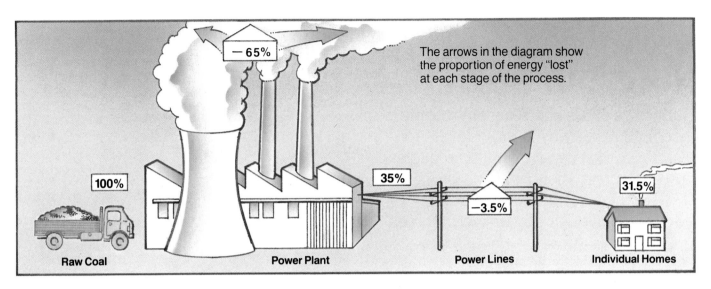

The arrows in the diagram show the proportion of energy "lost" at each stage of the process.

−65%

100% | 35% | −3.5% | 31.5%

Raw Coal | Power Plant | Power Lines | Individual Homes

IMPROVING EFFICIENCY, CUTTING POLLUTION AND CONSERVING ENERGY

Combined heat and power

'Combined Heat and Power (CHP) is the most energy-efficient method of turning fuel into useful energy. CHP works by making use of the heat produced in the process of electricity generation. Rather than dump heat into the atmosphere – as cooling towers at power stations do – it can be piped into buildings and factories and used. By this method the overall efficiency of electricity generation can be raised to 80 per cent or more. Increased efficiency means less fuel burned and, particularly where fossil fuels are used, less pollution. (David Green, Director of the UK Combined Heat and Power Association)

Energy from waste

Environmentalists believe that our energy policy should include building municipal waste incinerators which produce heat and power by burning rubbish. Already there is a large-scale refuse-fired CHP plant in Nottingham.

Waste-to-energy schemes also have economic advantages. In Paris, there are two large waste incineration plants which sell the heat that is produced. This helps to make the cost of disposing of Paris's waste among the lowest in France.

Cleaning up emissions

Coal-fired power stations produce 73 per cent of the sulphur dioxide and 35 per cent of the nitrogen oxides emitted into the atmosphere in Britain. Emissions of sulphur dioxide can be drastically reduced if the chimneys of a power-station are fitted with the cleaning apparatus called a flue gas desulphurization unit (FGD). These are expensive to fit, but are gradually being introduced. As more and more power stations are fitted with FGDs, so the amount of acid rain, produced by pollutants from power stations, will decrease.

Conserving energy

- 'Countries such as Britain and the United States use a lot of energy. An average family in the UK uses 80 times more energy than an average family in Africa.'
- Government figures (December 1989) show that the energy used in the United Kingdom could be reduced by 60 per cent by using fuels and electricity more efficiently.

Adapted from a Friends of The Earth fact-sheet

IN GROUPS

How can we reduce our energy use?

Insulate buildings.
Shower rather than bath.
Make fewer car journeys.
Support recycling schemes.
Buy the most efficient appliances.

Study the list of suggestions. Discuss how each of them would help to conserve energy. What other ways of conserving energy can you suggest?

Imagine you belong to an advertising agency. You have been given a budget of £3 million to produce a publicity campaign designed to promote energy conservation. You have to decide whether to target industries and businesses, schools and colleges or households. Produce a detailed plan, explaining who you plan to target, what messages you aim to get across and the methods you will use, e.g. leaflet/press and TV advertisements/a video.

IN PAIRS

Imagine you are managers/manageresses of a large company. Explain (**a**) how you would check that your factory and office buildings were using energy efficiently and (**b**) the instructions you would issue to all employees to make sure they are energy conscious.

NUCLEAR POWER – a risk worth taking?

During the 1960s and 70s many people thought that the way to provide cheap, clean electricity was by building nuclear power stations. Along with the USA, the USSR and Japan, Britain and France developed nuclear power programmes.

Then, in 1986 came the accident at Chernobyl, which blew a cloud of highly radioactive materials into the atmosphere and left the area around Chernobyl too contaminated with radioactivity for people to be able to live there. The cloud carried radioactive particles across Western Europe and some of them were carried to the earth in rain.

As a result, many people began to question the safety of the expanding nuclear programme. There were worries, too, about how to dispose of the highly radioactive waste produced by the reactors and what to do with the reactors themselves once they became too old to use. Also, studies showed that nuclear power was not as cheap as people had previously thought. It cost more to use nuclear power than power produced from coal or oil.

In Britain, and many other countries, the future for the nuclear power industry became uncertain. However, British Nuclear Fuels, which runs the nuclear reprocessing plant at Sellafield in Cumbria, believe that they could build a big new power station there that would produce electricity as cheaply as electricity from a coal-fired power station.

Those in favour of continuing the nuclear programme argue that nuclear power causes less pollution because it doesn't produce the gases that add to the 'greenhouse effect' and create 'acid rain'. Those against further development say it isn't worth the risk of another accident that might be far worse than the one at Chernobyl.

The Chernobyl reactor after the explosion, photographed (understandably) from a distance.

Nuclear accidents

October 1957. 1295 square kilometres of countryside contaminated by an explosion at Windscale in Cumbria.

March 1979. The nuclear reactor at Three Mile Island, Pennsylvania came close to a meltdown as a result of human error and mechanical failures.

March 1981. A tank at Tsurage nuclear reactor in Japan leaked radioactive waste water for several hours, polluting a nearby bay with radioactivity.

April 1986. Human error resulted in an explosion at the Chernobyl reactor, near Kiev in Ukraine.

DISPOSING OF NUCLEAR WASTE

Another major problem with nuclear power is the question of waste disposal. Radioactive waste has to be stored for anything from 100 to 100,000 years or more until it becomes inactive. There was a time when the sea was used for this waste disposal. Between 1967 and 1977 eight European countries dropped 46,000 tonnes of radioactive waste into the sea. Steel drums were used, each lined with reinforced concrete. These drums might have a life of about 300 years or so before they disintegrate. What happens to the radioactivity then? It will be several generations before we know. Most countries have now stopped using the ocean as a giant dustbin and instead favour deep burial of waste.

There is an alternative to dumping. Nuclear waste can be reprocessed to obtain plutonium, which can be used in fast breeder reactors. This is done at Sellafield in Cumbria already, and plans have been put forward to build a reprocessing plant at Dounreay in Scotland. Other countries will be delighted if we do. They can then ship their waste to us, we reprocess it and sell the plutonium. We then have the problem of getting rid of the waste that will still be left. For us this is a money-making enterprise. For other countries it is a way of disposing of a rather tricky problem.

Geo Magazine

For and against fission

Arguments about nuclear power have raged for decades. Some people think it is the great hope for the future; others believe it will destroy the planet.

The energy comes from uranium or plutonium. As the metal decays, it becomes radioactive and gives off heat which warms water. This water becomes steam, which then drives turbines to generate electricity.

If any substances contaminated by radioactivity escape, they can be highly dangerous. But are the risks really serious? We examine the facts below.

For

1 Carbon dioxide is a major contributor to global warming. Each unit of electricity produced by coal-fired stations releases 25 times more carbon dioxide than nuclear power stations.

2 Nuclear waste can be carefully contained in steel tanks, deep holes or shallow trenches. Nirex, the government waste disposal agency, is currently researching into depositaries located next to the UK plants.

3 Nuclear power may seem expensive, but the future of oil and coal prices is not secure. Oil prices may rise and could leave the cost of nuclear power relatively cheap.

4 Needing thousands of years to form, fossil fuels are being exploited at such a rate that supplies are dwindling fast. Oil reserves have 40 years left whereas it is estimated that uranium sources will last for another 5,000 years.

5 Safety regulations exist throughout the world. These were established by an international agreement.

Against

1 Although there's a one in a million chance of a repeat of the Chernobyl disaster, many incidents in the UK during the past few years have been potentially disastrous. This reveals the inefficiency of safety standards.

2 Generating only six per cent of the UK's total energy needs, 38,000 cubic metres of radioactive waste result from nuclear power stations. There are no effective ways of treating radioactive waste, which remains dangerous for thousands of years.

3 The financial cost of nuclear power often exceeds that of coal, oil and renewable energy.

4 Nuclear power was borne out of military research. Plutonium, a waste product of nuclear energy, is at the core of nuclear weapon explosions.

5 Renewable sources of energy are more environmentally sound. They have the potential to meet the world's total demands by the next century.

The Indy (11/10/90)

IN GROUPS

Would you work in the nuclear power industry?

'There are very strict safety rules and regulations. It's safer than several other industries.'

'What about these stories you read about the incidence of leukaemia being higher in areas close to nuclear power stations?'

'The media often carry scare stories about the nuclear power industry. But there's no conclusive proof. If there was, no one would work there, would they?'

'I'd rather work in the nuclear industry that not have a job.'

Discuss these views. Do you think the risks of working in the nuclear power industry are often exaggerated?

CLASS DISCUSSION

Organize a class debate on the motion 'This house believes that the risks of nuclear power outweigh the benefits and that the nuclear power programme should be gradually phased out.'

ROLE PLAY

You live in an area which is being considered as the site for a new nuclear power station or a new nuclear reprocessing plant. Make a list of local people who you think might be in favour of the proposal and of those who might oppose it. Role play a public meeting in which different people express views both for and against the proposal.

ENERGY WITHOUT END – renewable energy resources

Increasing the amount of energy you get from renewable energy resources would reduce atmospheric pollution and slow down the greenhouse effect. But the development of renewable resources is often expensive and all methods of producing energy have some environmental consequences.

Wind power

Specially designed windmills with propellers can produce electricity from a generator. But each windmill produces only small amounts, so a large number are required. The windmills are costly to build, so there is a large capital outlay, but they produce cheap electricity. Some people find windfarms unattractive, so their sites need to be chosen carefully. At present, less than 0.001 per cent of Britain's electricity is produced by wind power, but it is estimated that it could provide up to 20 per cent.

Hydro-electric power

The energy produced by falling water is used to turn a turbine and generate electricity. Hydro-electric power stations are expensive to build, but hydro-electric power is the cheapest form of electricity. In Britain, most of the suitable sites for large hydro-electric power stations have already been developed and they supply 1.6 per cent of our electricity. About 5.5 per cent of the world's electricity comes from hydro-electric power.

Biomass

Energy can be obtained by burning organic wastes. However, dealing with biofuels can be a major problem. One of the by-products of organic wastes is methane gas, which is highly explosive and contributes to the greenhouse effect. Environmentalists stress that only waste materials which cannot be recycled should be burnt and that they must be burnt cleanly, so that they do not pollute the air.

Wave power

The vertical movements of the waves are used to turn a generator and produce electricity. Various investigations have been carried out, but the technology for using wave power is undeveloped. However, since Britain has such a long coastline, wave power could be a potential source of power for our coastal towns and cities.

No large-scale schemes for harnessing wave power have been developed. One problem is the cost of development. Environmentalists are also concerned about the possible effects that disturbing the pattern of waves might have on marine life, on beaches and on the fishing industry.

Solar power

Solar power – the energy from the sun's heat – can be used to heat the space inside buildings and to heat water. Buildings can be designed so that windows allow in as much sunlight as possible. Also, they can be fitted with solar panels which collect the sun's energy and use it to heat water. Advantages of solar panels are that they need little maintenance, they do not produce any air or water pollution during manufacture and use, and they are made mainly from silicon, of which there is an abundant supply. In Britain, there is the potential for solar panels to make a significant contribution to the way we heat water, as their use becomes more widespread and the price drops.

Solar power can also be used to produce electricity by using the sun's light to produce energy in a photovoltaic cell. This method is still very expensive and there is not enough sunlight in Britain for them to have any real potential as sources of electricity. However, they are being developed by countries such as the USA and Japan, and power stations using solar cells to supply very large amounts of electricity are already being built.

Tidal power

The force of sea water can be used to turn turbines and generate electricity as the tide ebbs and flows. Large barriers, known as barrages, have to be built across a coastal inlet or an estuary, so the initial cost is high. But large amounts of electricity can be produced. The proposed scheme to build a barrage across the River Severn could supply 6–7 per cent of Britain's electricity needs and, at the same time, provide another road from England to Wales. But it would damage the habitat of the birds which live on the mud flats and could cause a build-up of pollution in the estuary.

Tidal power has been used in France, since the opening of the hydro-electric power station at the Rance estuary in 1967.

ROLE PLAY

You are a government energy committee. You have to decide how to spend £50 million pounds of government money to subsidize the development of renewable energy resources. Consider the advantages and disadvantages of each type of resource and decide how you would spend the money.

Act out a TV studio discussion in which a group of experts, each of whom is in favour of developing a particular resource, explain why they think we should invest in renewable energy.

IN PAIRS

Design and produce an information leaflet *The Energy Options* in order to make people aware of the different ways of producing the energy we need, the advantages and disadvantages of each method and of the choices that we each have to make.

Geothermal power

The heat from rocks inside the earth can be used to produce electricity by pumping water deep below the earth's surface. This produces steam which can be used to drive generators. In most parts of Britain, this would not be practicable because the hot rocks necessary to produce the steam are so deep below the surface. However, geothermal energy is already used in a number of countries, including New Zealand and Iceland.

FOR YOUR FILE

'Energy – the way forward – a personal view.' Write an article for a newspaper or magazine about how we can meet our energy needs and what you think the government's energy policy ought to be.

The National Health Service (NHS) was created in 1948. It aims to provide health care for everyone in Britain who needs it.

The cost of the NHS

The money to finance the NHS comes mostly from government funds – raised by taxation. The percentage of the nation's budget that is spent on the NHS and on other areas such as defence and education is decided by the government in power.

For a number of reasons, the cost of running the NHS has increased dramatically over the years. Developments in technology mean that hospitals have had to buy expensive new equipment. The cost of drugs has gone up. There has been a sharp rise in the number of elderly people in the population – the main group who rely on the NHS. Figures show that it costs the NHS four times as much to provide for the health needs of a person aged 65 to 74 as it does to provide for someone aged 16 to 64.

The problem for the government is how to control NHS costs while meeting people's health needs. During the 1980s, the Conservative government kept tight control of NHS spending. In order to save money, hospitals were forced to close wards and postpone operations. This led to long waiting lists and by 1992 there were over a million people waiting for NHS treatment. The average time they had to wait was 21 weeks.

Self-governing trusts

In order to try to produce a more cost-effective service, the Conservative government decided to reform the NHS. The reforms introduced in the National Health Service and Community Care Act, 1990 included allowing hospitals to become 'self-governing trusts' and to manage themselves rather than to be managed by the health authorities. The Act also enabled GPs to apply to become budget-holders and to manage their own finances.

A two-tier health service?

The Conservatives argued that this would introduce a limited amount of competition into health provision and force hospitals to improve services and be more efficient in order to attract patients. The Labour Party and the Liberal Democratic Party argued that the changes would produce a 'two-tier' health service and that they would lead to faster and better treatment for only some of the patients rather than all of the patients.

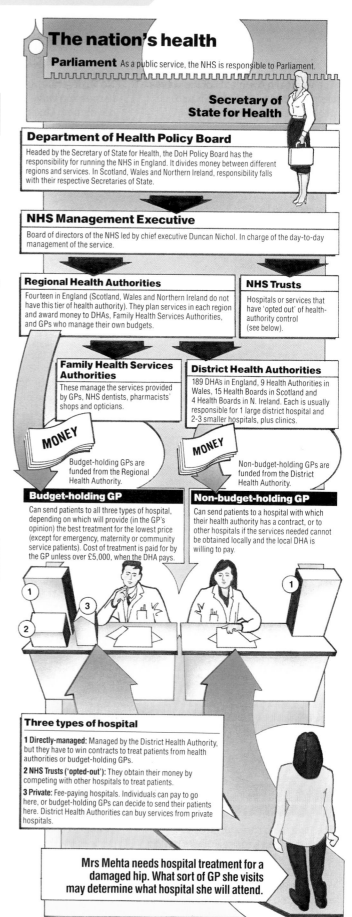

The nation's health

Parliament As a public service, the NHS is responsible to Parliament.

Secretary of State for Health

Department of Health Policy Board
Headed by the Secretary of State for Health, the DoH Policy Board has the responsibility for running the NHS in England. It divides money between different regions and services. In Scotland, Wales and Northern Ireland, responsibility falls with their respective Secretaries of State.

NHS Management Executive
Board of directors of the NHS led by chief executive Duncan Nichol. In charge of the day-to-day management of the service.

Regional Health Authorities
Fourteen in England (Scotland, Wales and Northern Ireland do not have this tier of health authority). They plan services in each region and award money to DHAs, Family Health Services Authorities, and GPs who manage their own budgets.

NHS Trusts
Hospitals or services that have 'opted out' of health-authority control (see below).

Family Health Services Authorities
These manage the services provided by GPs, NHS dentists, pharmacists' shops and opticians.

District Health Authorities
189 DHA's in England, 9 Health Authorities in Wales, 15 Health Boards in Scotland and 4 Health Boards in N. Ireland. Each is usually responsible for 1 large district hospital and 2-3 smaller hospitals, plus clinics.

MONEY Budget-holding GPs are funded from the Regional Health Authority.

MONEY Non-budget-holding GPs are funded from the District Health Authority.

Budget-holding GP
Can send patients to all three types of hospital, depending on which will provide (in the GP's opinion) the best treatment for the lowest price (except for emergency, maternity or community service patients). Cost of treatment is paid for by the GP unless over £5,000, when the DHA pays.

Non-budget-holding GP
Can send patients to a hospital with which their health authority has a contract, or to other hospitals if the services needed cannot be obtained locally and the local DHA is willing to pay.

Three types of hospital
1 Directly-managed: Managed by the District Health Authority, but they have to win contracts to treat patients from health authorities or budget-holding GPs.
2 NHS Trusts ('opted-out'): They obtain their money by competing with other hospitals to treat patients.
3 Private: Fee-paying hospitals. Individuals can pay to go here, or budget-holding GPs can decide to send their patients here. District Health Authorities can buy services from private hospitals.

Mrs Mehta needs hospital treatment for a damaged hip. What sort of GP she visits may determine what hospital she will attend.

How do we compare?

The National Health Service in France is, in theory, very similar to our own. People pay through their tax (six per cent of their wages, with employers paying twice as much) into a central pool, which funds the salaries of health workers and the cost of hospitals.

When people are sick, they pay for their treatment but the Securité Sociale reimburses up to 75 per cent of the bill.

At least half the country's population pays regular premiums to one of 7,000 insurance funds, known as mutuelles, which usually cover most of the difference – provided patients go to a public hospital or doctor with a fee structure agreed with the government. If patients want a doctor or specialist who charges above the government fee, they pay the extra themselves.

	FRANCE	BRITAIN
Population	55.62 million	55.78 million
Health budget	approx £75 billion	approx £30 billion
Doctors	114,534	31,854
Nurses and midwives	279,912	400,000
Hospital beds	622,522	408,700
Public spending as a percentage of total health spending	74.7	86.4
Private spending as a percentage of total health spending	25.3	13.6

In France, spending on health as a percentage of Gross Domestic Product is 8.7%. In Britain it is 5.8%. (This compares with 8.2% in Germany and 11.8% in the USA.)

A question of priorities

If you were in charge of the health service in your area, what would your priorities be? Study the list below, and number your priorities from 1–8. Then, form groups and compare your priorities with other people's and discuss how you made your decisions.

A   Closing a local maternity home in order to fund a new high technology maternity wing in a regional hospital.

B   Continuing to fund a unit working on 'test-tube' babies.

C   Improving the screening programme for breast cancer.

D   Funding a unit to carry out heart transplants.

E   Supporting research into drugs to treat AIDS.

F   Setting up local 'stop smoking' clinics.

G   Renovating the geriatric ward of a hospital.

H   Developing services to support people with disabilities living in the community.

Consider these views:

'Developing medical knowledge through research is vitally important.'

'We should always put the disadvantaged first.'

'Saving life must be the top priority, no matter what it costs.'

'Prevention is better than cure.'

IN PAIRS

In the USA, health services are provided primarily by private organizations. America relies heavily on the individual citizen being wealthy and responsible enough to take out a health insurance policy.

Should people in Britain be made personally more responsible for paying for their own health care as they are in the USA?

A room in a British private hospital.

FOR YOUR FILE

Carry out a survey to discover people's views on the National Health Service. Ask friends and relatives whether they are satisfied/dissatisfied with the service the NHS offers. What complaints do they have? What improvements would they like to see in the NHS? Are they for or against the NHS reforms that the Conservatives introduced in the National Health Services and Community Care Act, 1990? Write up a report of your findings and share it with other members of the class in either a group or class discussion.

Getting medical treatment

When you are ill, you are entitled to medical attention provided by the National Health Service.

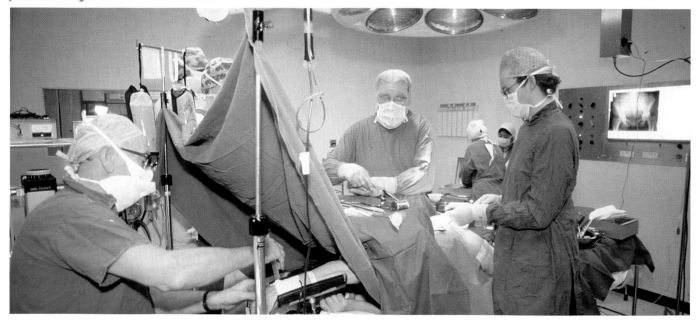

Finding a doctor

Everyone has a right to be on a doctor's list. If you are 16, you can choose your own doctor. Children under 16 have to go to a doctor chosen for them by a parent or a guardian. If you cannot find a doctor, the local Family Health Services Authority will find one for you.

- **You have the right to confidential treatment.**
- **You have the right to see your medical files.**
- **You have the right to see a practice leaflet telling you what services the surgery provides.**
- **You have the right to register with a different doctor for family planning.**
- **You have the right to change your doctor without stating a reason.**
- **You have the right to complain about your doctor.**

Hospital treatment

If you need hospital treatment, your doctor will discuss with you where you can go for treatment and recommend the hospital where you will receive the most appropriate care. To get hospital treatment you must be sent to the hospital by your doctor. However, if you have an accident, emergency treatment will be provided immediately and without question at a hospital casualty department.

If you are 16, you can give or refuse your consent to any surgical or medical care, but most hospitals require a parent's permission to perform operations on anyone under 18.

Family planning services

Family planning services are available from most doctors and from health authority family planning clinics. You can find the times of your nearest family planning clinic simply by looking in the telephone directory under 'Family Planning'. In addition to general sessions, some clinics offer sessions for particular groups – for example, young people. Family planning services are provided free and you do not need a doctor's letter before you go to a family planning clinic.

Services for women

Many doctors' surgeries run 'well-women' clinics which deal with issues to do with women's health. There is also a cervical cancer screening service, the aim of which is to detect conditions that could develop into cancer. If the conditions are found early enough, treatment is usually straightforward and nearly always effective.

About 2,000 women die from cervical cancer every year, so there is a programme designed to ensure that all women between the ages of 20 and 64 are invited for testing once every five years.

There is also a screening programme for breast cancer targeted at women over 50, since this is the age group with the highest incidence of breast cancer.

Charges

There is no charge for being seen by a doctor or for hospital treatment, but there is a charge for each item on a prescription. If you have to use drugs regularly, you can get a four-monthly or a yearly 'season ticket' from your local Family Health Services Authority.

Certain groups of people get free prescriptions: children under 16, pregnant women, people over retirement age, people claiming income support. If you have a road accident, doctors and hospitals can charge you for the treatment they give you. The fees have to be paid either by the drivers of the vehicles involved or their insurance companies.

Dental treatment

To obtain dental treatment you can either sign on with a dentist who still takes NHS patients or go to a private dentist. Your local Family Health Services Authority (Health Board in Scotland, Central Services Agency in Northern Ireland) keeps a list of NHS dentists.

Once you have joined a dentist's list as an NHS patient, you remain on the list so long as you continue to attend that dentist. But if you do not return for two years, or join another list, your arrangement with the first dentist ends.

When you receive NHS treatment, your dentist will discuss how much your treatment is going to cost after the initial examination and list the cost of each item on your Treatment Plan. There is a limit to how much you can be asked to pay. NHS dental treatment is free for:

- **children up to their 18th birthday**
- **students in full-time education up to their 19th birthday**
- **expectant and new mothers**
- **people on a low income**
- **those receiving Income Support or Family Credit or their adult dependants.**

Ophthalmic services

In the past, you used to be able to get a free eye-test from an optician. Now, only certain groups of people can still receive sight tests and eye examinations free under the NHS. Opticians do not have a list of registered NHS patients, so you can go to any optician you choose.

If you have a test and are told you need glasses, you will be given a form showing the power of lenses you require. You can either ask the optician to make the glasses for you, or take it to another optician to make them for you, or take it to a store or shop that sells spectacles. Depending on your circumstances, you may be entitled to an NHS voucher which you can put towards the cost of your glasses. Information about who is entitled to NHS vouchers can be obtained from your optician or the Family Health Services Authority.

Complaints

If you are not satisfied with aspects of your treatment, or services received, you should first discuss the problem with your doctor, dentist or optician. It is important to take the matter up promptly. If this proves unsuccessful, then contact the Family Health Services Authority who will explain the procedure for making complaints.

If you are not satisfied with hospital treatment, take the matter up with the hospital. If this does not resolve the issue, ask for a copy of the leaflet explaining how to make a complaint to the NHS authority.

IN GROUPS

Prepare a fact-sheet about the National Health Service giving essential information for people who are moving into your area. Include details of the local health centre and the clinics it runs as well as details of doctors, dentists, opticians and the nearest hospital with a casualty department. Think about the design of the fact-sheet and use a computer to produce a copy of it.

FOR YOUR FILE

A friend is planning to go abroad for a holiday. They wonder if they ought to take out medical insurance. Write a letter to the friend saying whether or not you think they should. (Points to consider: are they going to another EC country? What is form E111? Where can they obtain it?)

Choosing your friends

Afia

'When you are choosing friends first of all you notice the people who are loud and then you begin to see what people are really like, whether someone is kind, whether they have the same interests as you. From then you make friends with people that have something in common with you.

As far as I'm concerned I don't care what a person's background is as long as the person themselves is all right. The important thing is the person inside, that's what I'm looking at.'

Erica

'I like people who can think for themselves, not those who are always agreeing with you.'

Mumtaz

'I think it's better to have friends from the same background because you understand each other and trust each other more.'

Gillian

'When I first came to this school I was really loud and I used to go around with everyone. Now I've got many friends. A friend has got to be a laugh but then again, she's got to be loyal. She's got to respect me for what I am and me her.'

THE FIVE STAGES OF FRIENDSHIP

According to Drs Robert and Anne Delman of Harvard University in the USA, there are five stages of friendship:

STAGE 1 Selfish: Ages 3 to 7. During this stage, the main attraction is the friend's toys and other possessions.

STAGE 2 Obeying: Ages 4 to 9. How much friends get along together depends on how much one child is prepared to do what the other wants.

STAGE 3 'Give and take': Ages 6 to 12. Children start to understand that the friendship requires two-way effort, but their instincts towards their friends remain essentially selfish.

STAGE 4 Empathy: As they become teenagers, children develop greater emotional closeness. Friends begin to share their feelings and to confide their intimate secrets to each other.

STAGE 5 Equality: As adults, people develop friendships which are characterized by a need for both independence and mutual reliance.

IN GROUPS

Choosing friends

Discuss what Afia, Erica, Mumtaz and Gillian say about choosing friends. Do you think it's better to have friends from the same background?

What qualities do you look for in a person when you are considering whether or not they would make a good friend?

Close friendships

'The best thing about having a close friend is never having to pretend or put on an act. You can just relax and be yourself.' What do you consider to be the elements of a close friendship?

Is it possible for a girl and a boy to be close friends without becoming boyfriend and girlfriend?

How important do you think it is for everyone to have at least one close friend?

'Boys don't form as close friendships with each other as girls do, because boys are taught to think that men should be able to cope on their own, while girls are taught to express their feelings more openly and to share them.' Do you agree?

IN PAIRS

Discuss the twelve rules of relationships. In pairs, think of an example to illustrate each kind of behaviour and say why you believe that behaving in that way would help to reinforce and sustain a relationship.

FRIENDSHIP
the basic rules

On your own, consider the following situations, and write down which one of each pair of options you think you'd be more likely to follow.

1) Someone has done you a considerable favour. Do you:
a accept it gracefully, but not mention it again
OR
b make a special effort to pay them back – soon.

2) Imagine that you have just heard you're the winner of a magazine competition – a free holiday abroad. Do you:
a tell all your friends – immediately
OR
b feel shy about showing off, and only tell them when you're about to go away.

3) You realize that a friend is thoroughly miserable. Do you:
a leave them alone, on the grounds that no-one welcomes company when they're in this sort of mood
OR
b keep trying to contact them until they at least agree to talk to you.

4) You find yourself becoming increasingly irritated by a friend's habit of saying 'You know what I mean' after every utterance. Do you:
a tell them it's driving you crazy and then stop them every time they say it
OR
b tell yourself it's just a passing phase – and the price you pay for the pleasure of their company.

5) Someone you don't know particularly well tells you that your best friend has failed to repay some money. Do you:
a say there's probably a good reason why your friend hasn't paid the money back
OR
b agree that it's always wrong not to repay debts promptly.

6) You've had a hard day studying, and ring up a good friend to suggest meeting afterwards. They say they feel like spending the evening alone. Do you:
a accept that they probably have their reasons, and call up someone else instead
OR
b pull out all the stops to persuade them to come along.

7) A close friend tells you you've got to meet 'this fantastic person'. You do – and think they're terrible. Do you:
a tell yourself you could be mistaken
OR
b gently but firmly tell your friend exactly what you think.

8) At a party, you hear a friend who's had one drink too many boast about how they really told someone where to get off. Do you:
a quietly but firmly point out that they are exaggerating
OR
b smile to yourself and say nothing.

SCORING

Score your replies as follows:

Question 1:	a 1 point,	b	2 points.
Question 2:	a 2 points,	b	1 point.
Question 3:	a 1 point,	b	2 points.
Question 4:	a zero points,	b	2 points.
Question 5:	a 2 points,	b	1 point.
Question 6:	a 2 points,	b	1 point.
Question 7:	a 2 points,	b	zero points.
Question 8:	a zero points,	b	2 points.

The more points you have, the more valuable your friends are likely to find you. A score of 12 or more suggests that you are a pretty good friend to have about. At the other extreme, if you have a score of six or less, I suggest you read and then think of ways to implement the 12 rules of relationships.

1 Try to repay debts, favours and compliments
2 Share news of success with each other.
3 Show emotional support.
4 Volunteer help in time of need.
5 Try to make each other happy when you're together.
6 Trust and confide in each other.
7 Don't criticize each other in public.
8 Stand up for the other person when they're not there.
9 Be tolerant of each other's friends.
10 Don't nag.
11 Respect each other's privacy.
12 Accept that the occasional dispute is inevitable. Be prepared to negotiate and compromise – but not to grovel!

But above all, remember that however close you feel to someone, your friendship always needs to be worked at. After infancy, no relationship is ever easy, and no friends can be taken for granted – forever.

THE FOUR TYPES OF LOVE

Love is never a straightforward emotion, and it's complicated by the fact that there's not just one type of love. When someone says they're in love, they usually mean that they are experiencing a mixture of feelings drawn from the four different types of love.

ROMANTIC LOVE

Aaah, the stuff that Mills & Boon novels are made of!

Romantics dream of rose petal strewn duvets, champagne picnics by the river and declarations of undying love from a tall, dark, handsome partner who never experiences financial or sexual problems!

Maybe you *could* be the one in a million who finds a truly romantic, picture-book lover, but most people find that, even if their love affair starts out this way, the romance soon fades, to be replaced by arguments over who does the washing-up – sad, but true! Even sadder are people who are 'in love with being in love'. They are so desperate to find romance that they drift from partner to partner and often confuse sex with romantic love.

SEXUAL LOVE (i.e. LUST)

When you first meet you feel every symptom of falling deeply in love, your heart starts beating madly, you feel flushed and can't quite get your breath. Could this be love at first sight? When you do eventually get together, the sexual chemistry between you is so strong that every spare minute is spent snogging! Will this be a long and lasting love? Probably not. If you take a close look, you will doubtless see that the only thing holding your relationship together is sex. What you are experiencing is just good old-fashioned LUST. Nothing wrong with that, but don't fool yourself into believing you're 'in love'. When the sexual attraction dies, you'll probably find that you have nothing in common, and, contrary to your original opinion, you'll realize that you CAN live without each other.

OBSESSIVE LOVE

Obsession often develops when love is unrequited (one-sided). The obsessive person builds up the object of her/his affection to such an extent that she/he becomes a fantasy figure rather than a real person. Some go to crazy lengths to convince the other person of their 'love'. Hanging around their home, ringing at all hours of the day and night. What these people are really in love with is the *feeling* of being in love and the natural 'high' that it brings. But obsession can also happen *inside* relationships. If you find that your life revolves around someone who doesn't return your enthusiasm, but who you are convinced 'loves you in their own way' you'll only end up feeling rejected and hurt. Perhaps you feel all the pain of being in love, but have none of the warm tender moments? If this is the case, are *you* on the road to obsession?

PLATONIC LOVE

This is the type of love felt for parents, friends and relatives. It has nothing to do with sex, you simply care deeply for that person, it's as simple as that.

Platonic love is no less an emotion than sexual love, it just manifests itself in different ways. With a boyfriend/girlfriend, platonic love usually takes the form of security. You can go for ages without seeing them but when you do you fit easily into their conversation, have a really good laugh together and share your secrets. The thought of having a sexual relationship with a platonic friend never really crosses your mind, and platonic love is often the nicest form of love: comfortable, non-pressurizing and simple.

Adapted from *The Mizz Book Of Love*, Julie Burniston

What is love?

1 IS THERE SUCH A THING AS LOVE AT FIRST SIGHT?

'No, but I believe in *lust* at first sight!' (**Joe, 19**)

'Definitely. Especially when I've had a few drinks and I'm in a nightclub.' (**James, 21**) (*we think James might be pulling our leg here readers . . .*)

'Yes. I fell in love with my ex-husband at first sight and he moved in with me that very night! We married five months later but it was only gradually that I discovered his true nature, and the less said about that the better! My new boyfriend was love at first sight too, and I still feel the same – it's magic!' (**Tracey, 23**)

'I believe in chemistry which is a pretty good mimic. Chemistry is there from the first moment – but love comes after time and shared experiences.' (**Debbie, 17**)

2 DO YOU ONLY FALL *TRULY* IN LOVE ONCE IN A LIFETIME?

'I think your first love is one that you never forget and nothing afterwards really measures up to it.' (**Martin, 18**)

'No, otherwise people would never remarry after divorce or bereavement.' (**Helen, 16**)

'I'm in love at the moment and feel that if it ever broke up I would never love again . . . but I'm sure I would.' (**Clare, 19**)

3 IS IT POSSIBLE TO LOVE MORE THAN ONE PERSON AT A TIME?

'No way. Being in love means giving all your time, loving and energy to one special person – you can't split it.' (**Craig, 22**)

'You can love them for different reasons but it couldn't be very strong love.' (**Liz, 17**)

'Not for me, but maybe it's possible for other people.' (**Jenny, 19**)

4 WHAT IS THE DIFFERENCE BETWEEN LOVING SOMEONE AND BEING 'IN LOVE' WITH THEM?

'Being 'in love' is the initial honeymoon stage, where everything is passionate and perfect. Once this passion cools and the infatuation wears off it's replaced by love, a deeper, stronger feeling altogether.' (**Pauline, 18**)

'Loving someone is knowing all their faults and still wanting to go on seeing them – being in love is thinking they are perfect and not even seeing their faults!' (**Lesley, 20**)

'Loving is a long-term feeling built on trust. Being in love is passion, the shakes, infatuation.' (**David, 21**)

5 IS IT POSSIBLE TO GO THROUGH LIFE WITHOUT EVER FALLING IN LOVE?

'I think it's possible, but it's a denial of a basic human feeling.' (**Jane, 15**)

'I hope not, for everyone's sake, but some people must do.' (**Sam, 14**)

'No. Everyone falls in love with something, whether it be another person of the same sex, God or even themselves!' (**Lynn, 18**)

6 AND FINALLY . . . WHAT IS YOUR DEFINITION OF TRUE LOVE?

'Giving your all to someone without expecting anything back.' (**Diane, 17**)

'Total trust, telepathy, attraction, humour and most of all, patience.' (**Chris, 19**)

'Caring more about that person than you do about yourself.' (**Milly, 15**)

'Being on the same wavelength, trust, honesty and knowing that someone's always there for you.' (**Carl, 22**)

'Love is as indefinable as it is unique between individuals . . .' (**Sue, 20**)

Adapted from *The Mizz Book Of Love*, Andrew Wilson

IN GROUPS

Discuss the questions and the answers people gave. Get someone in the group to note down the different views of the people in your group, then share your ideas in a class discussion.

On your own write down the main things you would hope for from a romantic relationship, then compare your ideas in a group discussion. Do you think a girl expects different things from a romantic relationship than a boy does?

THE PRESSURE TO CONFORM

Be it from parents, friends, the media or even advertising slogans, there's often a lot of pressure on girls to have a boyfriend. Girls are often made to feel that they must have a man in tow in order to be socially acceptable. This is silly! Although attitudes have changed, there is still a lot of prejudice against anyone who doesn't fit into the 'normal' category and whenever a girl does something not expected of her, such as remaining single, she is labelled 'odd' or 'abnormal' and treated dismissively or even abusively. Then she often receives the insult that's hurled at all girls who step outside the traditional role model – 'lesbian'. The fact that it's used as an insult implies that women who prefer the company of other women to men must be weird! Society's pressure towards a coupledom can make some girls feel incomplete, lacking. But it's time we all forgot the absurd idea that the only attachments worth forming are those with potential boyfriends and positively *enjoy* being single.

Just Seventeen (30/3/88)

IN PAIRS

Discuss the article, 'The pressure to conform.' Do you think too much pressure is put on teenage girls and boys to form relationships and become couples?

Talk about the ways (**a**) parents and relatives, (**b**) friends, (**c**) the media put pressure on teenagers to find a partner. Suggest ways of dealing with such pressures.

MAKE OR BREAK
what makes relationships work?

BREAKING POINTS

What makes relationships break down? Below is a list of some of the reasons why relationships break down. Read through it and give each reason a score from 0–16 to show how often you think that reason is the cause of a relationship between two young people breaking down (0 = never; 16 = extremely often). If you can think of other reasons why teenage relationships break down, add them to your list and give them a score. When you have finished, compare your answers and share your ideas with other people in a group discussion.

A Not being able to talk together easily.

B Jealousy – either sexual, or of the other person's activities and friends.

C Parental objections to the relationship.

D Quarrels and arguments.

E One partner becoming 'clingy' or too dependent on the other.

F One partner gossiping about the relationship to their friends.

G Too much expectation of sexual intimacy, and pressure to 'go the whole way'.

H One partner being 'unfaithful' and going out with someone else.

I Being insensitive to the needs and wishes of the other person.

J Not being able to get on with the other person's friends.

K Boredom.

L Feeling tense when you're together – feeling it's 'not right'.

M One partner dominating the other.

N Lack of personal self-confidence.

O Moody behaviour.

P Feeling that things are getting 'too serious, too soon'.

Donna's Story

'I'd been going out with my boyfriend for six months and then he went on holiday with his mates. While he was away someone I knew had a party. I nearly didn't go, but in the end I decided to make the effort. I'd been there about an hour when this boy walked in and I couldn't stop thinking how handsome he was. I noticed that he kept looking at me and then suddenly he came over and asked me if I was on my own. I said yes, and although I knew I should say my boyfriend was away, I didn't. We ended up kissing and he asked me out. Although I felt a bit guilty, it was flattering and exciting to have someone to flirt with. We arranged to meet two days later and I went home with a huge smile on my face. The next day I woke up feeling like a naughty child, but it was a good feeling. Then that afternoon my boyfriend rang me saying that he missed me and couldn't wait to come home. That was it. I felt terrible and decided not to turn up for my date. I never heard from the boy at the party again but I didn't tell my boyfriend about him. What he doesn't know can't hurt him.'

Just Seventeen

IN PAIRS

Discuss Donna's story. Donna says: 'What he doesn't know doesn't hurt him.' Do you agree? Was it fair of Donna not to tell her boyfriend? If you were Donna's boyfriend and she explained what had happened and how she felt about it, how would you react?

Are there certain personal things that you should be able to keep private and never tell your partner? Is it all right for each of you to have secrets? Are there certain things you should always tell your partner, even though it may be upsetting or embarrassing to do so?

Discuss Heather's story. Is it wrong of friends to expect you to talk to them about your relationships? What things is it all right to tell friends about your relationship? What kind of things should you avoid talking to them about?

Heather's Story

'I can't believe how stupid I was. But this was two years ago. I like to think I've grown up now.

'I was going out with this boy called Nick. He was shy, but I got to know him really well and he opened up to me. We used to talk for hours about things in our lives. I was never into analysing things before I met Nick, but he changed all that. I still kept my girlfriends, though, and we used to go out and have a laugh.

'Then one day we stayed up ages talking and he told me just how much he loved me. The next time I went out with a bunch of mates I got a bit drunk and told them that Nick had admitted he loved me. It all got out of hand because people just passed the rumour on and changed the story to make it sound really slushy and silly. It got back to Nick and he couldn't believe that I'd turned an intimate moment into a funny story. We split up and I felt so miserable. I knew it was all my fault.'

The Mizz Book Of Love

What makes a relationship grow?

Read through the list below and give each idea a score according to how much you think it helps to make a relationship grow (0 = not at all; 10 = a great deal). Add any other ideas of your own and give them a score, then share your views in a group discussion.

1 Making sure you always look your best.

2 Sharing the same interests.

3 Being able to have fun together.

4 Being able to talk about personal things together, and listen to each other.

5 Agreeing how far you want the relationship to develop sexually.

6 Being able to argue and have differences in a friendly way.

7 Getting on with each other's friends.

8 Trusting each other.

9 Allowing each other to keep some things secret.

10 Giving in to whatever your partner suggests.

11 Tolerating each other's irritating habits.

12 Each going out on your own sometimes.

13 Getting on with your own lives in positive ways.

14 Not trying to control each other.

IN PAIRS

What causes arguments between teenage couples? Make a list of the things that a teenage couple might quarrel about. Then, choose one of them and either develop role plays or write scripts that show two different ways of handling the quarrel so that it (a) remains unresolved, (b) is sorted out.

Do you think that teenagers argue about different things to older couples?

FOR YOUR FILE

'*Looking back, I can see why it didn't work out.*' Write a diary entry in which a teenager looks back on a relationship and explains the reasons why it didn't work out.

IN GROUPS

Dealing with disagreements

What's the best way to deal with arguments and quarrels? Below is a list of different types of behaviour. Discuss which approaches you think are most likely to help solve arguments and quarrels.

- Shouting.
- Losing your temper.
- Arguing and trying to win.
- Trying to manipulate the other person.
- Trying to please the other person.
- Crying.
- Refusing to talk about it.
- Sitting down to talk it through.
- Finding someone to help the two of you sort it out.
- Letting the matter drop.

Q What is a trade union?

A A trade union is an association of employees who have joined together to protect and promote their interests by negotiating jointly with their employers. The process of negotiation between a trade union and an employer or an employers' organization is known as collective bargaining.

Q How many trade unions are there?

A In 1992, there were 323 trade unions in the United Kingdom. Just over 8.4 million people were members of trade unions – about 44 per cent of the working population.

The six biggest unions together had over 5 million members and a further 13 unions all had more than 100,000 members. At the other end of the scale are some very small unions with less than 1,000 members.

Q What different types of trade unions are there?

A There are four types of union:
- General workers unions, which represent workers of all kinds, both skilled and unskilled, from a range of industries, e.g. The Transport and General Workers Union.
- Craft unions, which represent workers with a particular skill from a group of industries, e.g. sawmakers.
- Industrial unions, which represent workers of all kinds, both skilled and unskilled, in a particular industry, e.g. all those employed in the shipbuilding industry.
- White collar unions, which represent people in non-manual occupations, e.g. teachers.

Q How are unions funded?

A By the members. When you join a union, you pay a weekly subscription. The amount you pay depends on which union you join and how much you are being paid. In 1992, the average union subscription was £1–6 per week.

Q How are unions organized?

A The members of a union who work in the same place or live in the same area form a local branch of the union. Each branch elects its own union representative to act as their spokesperson. This person is often known as the shop steward.

The members of large unions also elect regional officials and a national executive – a committee of leaders which acts on behalf of the members. The national executive is often chosen at the union's annual conference. This conference involves delegates from all of the branches.

Q What is the TUC?

A TUC stands for the Trades Unions Congress, which is a voluntary association of independent unions. At the beginning of 1992, it consisted of 72 unions representing 8,192,664 workers. The main job of the TUC is to encourage unions to work together and to help them to achieve together what they are unable to do alone. It draws up common policies on matters of importance to people at work and presents them to the government, to employers' associations, such as the Confederation of British Industry (CBI) and to international bodies, such as the European Community.

Why join a union?

Unions exist to protect people at work. Even in the best run workplaces problems arise from time to time. It is then that workers need someone to turn to – someone who knows about legal rights, who can take up an individual case or speak on behalf of all workers and someone who has the backing of a national organization. Polls show most people believe unions are essential to protect workers' interests.

(Norman Willis, TUC General Secretary)

'What will a union do for me?'

- Negotiate with your boss about pay, hours of work, and holidays; about the way that wages are paid, about allowances, extra payments and about retirement and pension arrangements.

- Represent you if you have difficulty with your employer. For example, if you believe you've been treated badly, disciplined unfairly or keep complaining about a problem which nobody seems to do anything about.

- Negotiate to improve your working conditions. For example, you may be exposed to health and safety hazards, such as toxic fumes or unguarded machinery, or there may be poor washing and toilet facilities and inadequate fire precautions.

- Negotiate to protect you if you are under threat of redundancy or lay-off.

- Help with national insurance matters.

- Ensure that part-time workers receive fair treatment. As a member you may also be entitled to other benefits, such as legal advice and representation, a range of cash benefits and other services, and opportunities to attend union education courses.

Adapted from *Why Join A Union?*, a TUC leaflet

IN GROUPS

Is it worth joining a trade union? Will you definitely join a trade union when you start work or will it depend on what job you get?

Organize a survey. Interview a number of people to find out whether or not they belong to a trade union. Ask them why they decided to join or not to join a union and what union members think are the benefits of belonging to a union. Begin by working together to draw up the questionnaire you are going to use. Choose someone to analyse the results of the survey and to report the findings to the rest of the class in a class discussion.

ROLE PLAY

Use the information contained in this unit to act out a scene in which a union representative explains to a young worker the benefits of joining a trade union. Before you begin, carefully note down any information you feel may be of use to you during your role play.

FOR YOUR FILE

A friend of yours is about to start a job. They cannot decide whether or not to join a union. Write a letter telling them your views on union membership.

The right to strike?

A LAST RESORT?

Trade unions say the right to strike is an essential weapon to be used in the last resort when bargaining or arbitration has broken down. However, argument still rages over whether some strikes are morally justifiable. Some people – union members amongst them – believe that the right of patients to medical care should take absolute priority over the right of health workers to strike. Striking teachers have been accused of sacrificing children's interests to their own. Some union members, however, argue that unless workers in these services strike for improvements, patient care and education will both suffer.

A QUESTION OF MORALITY?

There is disagreement too over whether unions should have the right to strike. During the two World Wars there were legal restrictions on the right to strike, but stoppages took place none the less. Currently, the armed forces and police are forbidden to go on strike, and some would extend the ban to members in essential services such as fire officers and health workers. The TUC itself believes that 'special steps have to be taken to avoid disruption to services on which the community relies.' However, they say that these should be based, not on legal curbs of the right to strike, but on high standards of industrial relations.

The Role Of Trade Unions,
Brigid McConville

During 1984–85 thousands of miners went on strike because the Coal Board planned to close pits, which it said were uneconomical. There were violent clashes between the government, police and working miners. During the course of the strike, there were around nine thousand arrests and two miners were killed on picket lines. After 12 months, the strike ended in defeat for the miners.

FOR YOUR FILE

1 What new laws did the Tory government pass between 1979 and 1992 to curb union powers?

2 Explain the new style of industrial relations which Japanese car firms have introduced.

Curbing the power of the unions

Since 1979 the unions have had much less freedom to take industrial action. One of Margaret Thatcher's main election pledges that year was to curb union power.

The Government has done this by passing new laws. Unions now have to hold a secret vote among their members before they strike. They must also vote to choose new leaders, and to decide if they will send money to support political parties. During a strike, they are allowed to place only six members outside the workplace to try and persuade other workers from breaking the strike by going to work – an activity known as 'picketing'. Secondary action – where one group of workers strikes to support another – has been virtually eliminated. And employers have been given new legal powers to prevent unions striking, or to claim financial penalties from them if they do.

The latest Employment Bill [now passed], aims to end the 'closed shop'. This is a system found mainly in the road haulage, printing, and shipping industries, and in the acting profession, which prevents people from being employed if they do not belong to a certain union. About 2.6 million workers are in closed shops today.

The *Education Guardian*
(11/9/90)

Towards a striking new image

Strikes are only a small part of trade union activity but unions have had much less freedom to take industrial action under Margaret Thatcher.

The image that many people have of trade unions is of striking miners clashing with the police during the 1984/5 miners strike, or of print workers at Wapping in 1986.

But few strikes, in fact, end in violence. Indeed strikes, and other forms of industrial action, are only a small part of trade union activities. Most union members never go on strike.

Last year about four million days of work were lost through strikes, down from an average of 13 million in the 1970s. About 30 times as many days were lost last year through absence – people staying at home due to sickness, injury, or not turning up.

The threat of a strike is a unions most powerful weapon. Unions were founded on the principle that , by collectively removing their labour, workers could force employers to give them better pay, or safer working conditions.

But over the last 10 years unions have tried to emphasise the variety of other roles they perform, in an attempt to shrug off their old strike-bound image. They have stressed their role in improving health and safety conditions in the workplace. Last year, 697 people died at work, and more than 34,000 were seriously injured. Workers in the North Sea have been in dispute this summer because they want their union to be recognised. They say this would allow them to enforce safety regulations on the oil rigs.

Unions are also developing new financial services for their members, including pensions discount schemes and insurance. In May, the union movement launched its own credit card – Unity First Mastercard. Many unions have agreed to change the way their members work, to match changes in technology. They have accepted more flexible hours and working practices, often in exchange for higher pay.

The most radical of these changes are no-strike and single-union agreements. Some employers, particularly in newly-built Japanese car factories, will only recognise one union in the workplace and will only make agreements with that one union.

Toyota, Sony and Toshiba have asked unions in their factories to sign no-strike agreements. If there is a dispute, workers and managers will not negotiate with each other in the normal way. Instead, the dispute is brought before ACAS, the arbitration service. This is a body of independent experts, mainly academics, whose job it is to decide how the dispute should be resolved. Both sides must agree to accept the decision of ACAS.

There are now about 40 no-strike agreements in this country. But they cover only about 15,000 workers. No-strike agreements cannot, in any case, be fool-proof, because it is impossible to prevent workers striking if they want to. According to the London School of Economics, there have been at least three recent strikes in factories covered by such agreements.

Nevertheless, the changes within the work-force suggest that relations between employers and unions have improved since the 1979 'Winter of Discontent', when the Labour government lost the General Election in the wake of a series of strikes. A survey last year showed that more than two thirds of employers thought unions played an important role in their companies, and more than half thought their relations with the unions had improved over the past 10 years.

THE Nissan car factory in Sunderland is an indication of a new style of industrial relations that has been imported from Japan in recent years. The company, which has Japanese directors but only British workers on the factory floor, has attempted to avoid an 'us and them' attitude which is common in UK manufacturing. There is no traditional division between Nissan 'management' and 'workers'. Everyone uses the same car park and canteen, has the same sickness scheme and perks. There is only one union allowed In the plant – the Amalgamated Engineering Union (AEU), which represents about 35 per cent of the staff. Workers elect representatives to a Company Council to deal with their problems.

The Education Guardian (11/9/90)

Trade Unions and politics

Trade unions try to promote their members' interests by acting as pressure groups. For example, they may lobby the government to introduce legislation that will improve the rights of individual workers. They also try to influence the government to adopt economic policies that will benefit their members.

Many unions have a political fund which they use to support a political party and for other pressure group activities. Unions which have a political fund must hold regular ballots to ensure that their members are in favour of having such a fund.

Trade unions also act as pressure groups to try to bring about change on political issues that do not directly affect their members. For example, trade unions have been very active in campaigning for the rights of black people in South Africa by supporting the anti-apartheid movement.

IN GROUPS

Talk about why trade unions seek to influence governments. If you belonged to a trade union, would you vote for or against having a political fund? Explain why.

'Trade unions should stick to matters which directly concern their members and not get involved in other issues.' Do you agree with this statement?

IN PAIRS

The position of trade unions in other countries varies. In some countries, such as West Germany, the union movement is strong and powerful. In other countries, trade unionists are persecuted and imprisoned. Amnesty International, the human rights organization, reports that among the thousands of prisoners of conscience throughout the world there are many trade unionists.

Choose another country. How strong is the trade union movement in that country? How are trade unionists treated there? Prepare a fact-sheet about trade unions in that country for a wall display.

WHAT DO PEOPLE THINK OF TRADE UNIONS?

Trade union membership has declined in recent years from its peak of 12 million members in 1979, partly due to rising unemployment and partly due to changing patterns of employment.

There is no doubt that trade unions have received adverse media publicity in recent years. Critics argue that trade unions make excessive wage claims that are primarily responsible for inflation and for pricing workers out of jobs. Criticisms have also been made of undemocratic elections, and in order to overcome this charge unions now have to elect their leaders by secret ballot.

Others argue that unions have become too powerful and should have their 'wings clipped'. Some think that workers in vital industries such as power and transport should not be allowed to join unions because of the possible effect on public safety if they went on strike. Workers at GCHQ, the government communications and surveillance centre, are no longer allowed to be members of any union.

Another charge frequently levelled at unions is that they undermine the competitiveness of British industry because of restrictive practices and opposition to technological progress. However, a survey by ACAS in 1988 of 650 employers showed that 'the presence of trade unions has not appeared to inhibit the introduction of new working practices'.

Supporters of trade unions argue that they are essential for protecting the interests of employees who might otherwise get a raw deal from powerful employers or in industries which are declining and where redundancies are highly likely. Unskilled workers can be in a particularly weak position.

Unions played an active part in persuading the government to pass the Health and Safety at Work Act. They also offer a range of personal services, legal advice, training, protection against unfair dismissal, and accident and sickness benefits, and can attempt to influence government policy by political lobbying, particularly through the TUC.

There has also been a small number (only about forty-five in the UK up to 1989) of new-style agreements signed between employers and unions, involving single-union deals and no-strike clauses. Their importance for attracting foreign investment cannot be overestimated at a time when many international companies still perceive Britain's record of industrial unrest with suspicion.

Some observers argue that these new-style agreements, such as the one at Toshiba UK's plant in Plymouth point the way forward for a new era of industrial relations in Britain.

IN GROUPS

List five advantages and five disadvantages of trade unions. Use the points mentioned in the article and, if necessary, add any other points you can think of. Then, discuss each statement in turn and decide whether or not you agree with it. Appoint someone to act as spokesperson to report your views to the rest of the class.

FOR YOUR FILE

Choose a trade union. Find out all you can about how it is organized and what its aims are. Does it support a political party? If so, how? What pressure group activities (if any) has it been involved in recently?

How healthy is your lifestyle?

We'd all like to think that we're reasonably fit and healthy, but just how much do you really know about looking after yourself? Not eating the right things and taking too little exercise now could lead to problems later on. So where do you fit in? Do you know what's good for you?

A healthy attitude, a healthy body

There is growing medical evidence to suggest that features of an unhealthy lifestyle, such as smoking, consuming too much alcohol, not getting enough exercise and an unhealthy diet, are important contributory factors in the development of many life-threatening illnesses, such as heart disease and some cancers. Avoiding such illnesses depends more on your attitude than anything else. First of all, you need to identify which parts of your lifestyle need changing and then decide how you are going to go about changing them. The effects of an unhealthy lifestyle are likely to build up over the years, so the longer you put off doing something to change your lifestyle, the more chance there is that some damage will already have been done. For example, if you are someone who eats too much fat, then it is possible that there already may be fatty deposits building up inside your arteries. (Fatty streaks have been found in the arteries of children as young as ten.) These fatty deposits are one of the earliest indicators of heart disease and could, in time, increase so that they ultimately cause either a heart attack or stroke. Making up your mind to lead a healthy lifestyle now is the best way of protecting yourself against developing these diseases in the future.

IN PAIRS Opposite are 15 statements. On your own at first, write down whether you think they are TRUE or FALSE. Check the answers, then tell your partner how you scored and discuss what you have learned from the quiz about what makes a healthy diet and about the importance of regular exercise.

FIT FOR LIFE?.............

1 It is healthier to avoid additives than to eat less fat, sugar and salt, and more fibre.

2 A can of non-diet cola contains approximately seven teaspoons of sugar.

3 An average rump steak contains more fibre than a tin of baked beans.

4 We all need some sugar in the diet to provide energy.

5 White bread is good for you.

6 Fast food is always unhealthy.

7 Aerobic exercise keeps your heart fit.

8 Walking is an aerobic exercise.

9 We now know jogging is bad for the heart.

10 You must exercise daily to keep fit.

11 Exercise is only important as you get older.

12 It's useful to exercise when you are under stress.

13 Smokers are just as likely to die from getting run over as from actually smoking.

14 Even one cigarette a day can harm you.

15 You should always make sure that you eat some food containing Vitamin C every day.

Three golden rules

No matter how well you scored, everyone will benefit from following these basic guidelines:

- Eat less fat, sugar and salt, and more fibre.
- Aim to have three 20-minute sessions of aerobic exercise each week (e.g. swimming, cycling, skipping, disco dancing, running).
- Don't smoke.

.How did you do?...............

For questions 1, 3, 4, 6, 9, 10, 11 and 13 score 3 points if you answered 'false', and 1 point if you answered 'true'. For questions 2, 5, 7, 8, 12, 14 and 15, score 3 points if you answered 'true', and 1 point if you answered 'false'.

1 False. The key to healthy eating is consuming less fat, sugar and salt and more fibre. It just so happens that many foods which are high in fat and sugar – like cakes and biscuits – also often contain additives.

2 True. Fresh unsweetened fruit juice is a healthy alternative.

3 False. Meat contains no fibre. Fibre is only found in food of plant origin – grains, fruit, vegetables and pulses (peas, beans, etc).

4 False. We can obtain energy from protein, fat and complex carbohydrates like potatoes and pasta. There is no need to eat sugar at all.

5 True. White bread is a good source of fibre, though wholemeal and granary breads are better. 'Softgrain' white loaves have added extra fibre.

6 False. Beans on toast, take-away jacket potatoes, stir fries, and pizzas which are low in high fat ingredients are all healthy fast food meals. However, watch out for doner kebabs and burgers and chips, which are heavy on fat.

7 True. Aerobic exercise is exercise which keeps your heart, lungs and circulation in good shape. It improves your stamina. However, you should always work to a sensible training programme to avoid placing too much stress on your muscles and joints.

8 True. Brisk walking can be excellent aerobic exercise.

9 False. Jogging is good for your heart *providing* you don't overdo it and work to a sensible training programme for your personal level of fitness.

10 False. Experts recommend that adults take a minimum of three 20-minute sessions of any aerobic exercise a week – try swimming, brisk walking, running or cyling to keep fit.

11 False. Exercise is important to people of all ages.

12 True. When you are under stress your body reacts as if you are facing a physical danger and switches on the 'fight or flight' response. This means it gears up for action, so exercise is beneficial and can help release tension.

13 False. The Royal College of Physicians says that out of a thousand smokers, six may die in road accidents but 250 will die from smoking-related disease.

14 True. Figures show that regular smoking (one cigarette or more per day) can greatly increase the risk of dying from a heart attack.

15 True. Fresh fruit and vegetables are good sources of Vitamin C, which is essential, especially when you're under stress. The body cannot store it, so you should always include a portion of fruit or fresh vegetables in your daily diet.

SCORING

37–45: Congratulations! You've got an excellent understanding of the principles of personal health and how to put them into practice.

26–36: You probably know most of the basic principles of looking after your health, but aren't so sure about putting them into practice.

15–25: You're quite confused and need to brush up on the basics. But there's no need to panic. Follow our three golden rules, pay attention to our tips for a healthy attitude, and these, together with your own common sense, should point you in the right direction.

Cultivating a healthy attitude

A healthy lifestyle doesn't mean giving up all the good things in life. It's the little things that can make a big difference.

- Cycle or walk to school. If it's too far, get off the bus a stop earlier and walk (providing it's safe to do so).
- Join a dance or aerobics class or take up a sporting activity. If you don't like traditional sports, what about roller-skating or the martial arts?
- Become a food label watcher. Remember that manufacturers have to list the ingredients in most foods in descending order of weight, with the heaviest first. Watch out for those where fat, salt and sugar come high on the list.
- Substitute semi-skimmed or skimmed milk for the full fat variety. This can make an enormous difference to your fat intake.
- Try to eat a portion of vegetables or salad at least once a day.
- Substitute fruit for fatty and sugary snacks like crisps and biscuits.
- Drink fresh unsweetened fruit juice. It's full of vitamins and more refreshing than fizzy soft drinks (which often contain additives).
- Build up a repertoire of healthy, easy to prepare meals – heat-and-serve pizzas, baked beans on toast, baked potatoes.
- When making sandwiches use granary bread. Use a low-fat spread rather than butter, or substitute it with a little low-calorie mayonnaise.

IN PAIRS Work with a friend. Use the information on these pages to help you to design an attractive and informative leaflet for people of your own age intended to convey the message 'Keep Fit, Eat Wisely, Stay Healthy'.

Drinking and drugs - it's your choice

Young 'drink to reduce pressure'

YOUNG PEOPLE are turning to drink to escape examination and work pressures, according to a report published yesterday.

The survey questioned 874 teenagers and adults in their early 20s about their drinking habits.

Comments "appear to indicate that for some of them, alcohol is seen as a way of reducing the stress or coping with the pressure of their jobs or school", it says.

All those who took part started drinking before they were 18, of which 58 per cent started drinking before they were 14.

It also found that 16 per cent drank for no reason other than to get drunk, and 10 per cent drank four times or more a week. The effect of alcohol on their health worried about 28 per cent, and 25 per cent of under-18s who drank regularly wanted to drink less.

Although 61 per cent drank only once a week or less, the survey and youth workers confirmed "that there is concern, both by young people and the wider community, about the part alcohol plays in the life of young people".

The survey adds: "Some young people drink to excess and then behave irresponsibly. But the enforcement of current legislation would appear to be able to deal with this issue."

Nearly all young people (96 per cent) said drinking did not affect them at school or work, but 11 per cent had had to take time off because of hangovers. The most popular places to drink were pubs and the home — though 2 per cent said they drank at school.

After drinking, 10.5 per cent of boys and young men said they felt violent and 11.5 per cent felt brave, while 26 per cent of males and 18 per cent of females felt "randy".

The Independent (11/9/90)

NAME G PARSONS
D.O.B. 09-06-68
1812345

Whether or not your lifestyle includes habits such as smoking, drinking or taking drugs is up to **you**. There may be circumstances in which other people put pressure on you to try a substance. But in the end it's your decision. After all, it's your body you may be putting at risk, not theirs.

IN GROUPS

Study the article *Young 'drink to reduce pressure'*, then discuss these questions.

Why do young people drink alcohol? List all the reasons you can think of. Which are the main reasons?

Why do some young people drink to excess? What do you think of (**a**) adults, (**b**) teenage girls, (**c**) teenage boys who get drunk? Are you worried about the effects that alcohol can have on your health?

Are young people who don't want to drink under any pressure to do so?

What do you think of people who drink and drive?

Do you think ID cards should be used in pubs/off-licences to prove your age? Do you think people who drink are more likely to get into trouble with the law?

If you thought that a friend had started to drink too much, what would you do? List all the things you could do and decide what action you would probably decide to take.

ROLE PLAY

A group of you have been to a disco. The person who is driving you home has been drinking. One of you says that they are not going to be driven home by someone who has been drinking. The others put pressure on them to get into the car. Role play the scene. Take it in turns to be the person who is refusing to be driven home. How easy was it to resist the pressure of the group and say no? What arguments did you use?

Some facts you should know

▶ **DRINK AND SEX**
There's nothing attractive about a drunk. Heavy drinking can seriously damage your sexual ability. Too much alcohol can make it difficult to conceive a baby. Drink can also lead to careless sexual behaviour.

▶ **DRINK DRIES YOU UP**
Alcohol dehydrates your body – one of the reasons for that horrible hangover feeling. The water is pushed out of your cells by the alcohol and builds up in your blood. It's bad for your skin, and leads to wrinkles and a puffy face.

▶ **DEATH AND ACCIDENTS**
More than 1,000 men die each year in road accidents involving drink. Alcohol also causes accidents at work and in the home.

▶ **ARE YOU SPOILING A GOOD LIFE**
You may be enjoying yourself drinking – but think of your family and friends. Many rows are caused by too much drinking. Don't risk hurting those you care about. Alcohol also plays a part in unlawful behaviour. Nearly half of violent crimes are committed by people who have been drinking.

Drugs - what's your attitude?

'Avoid places where drugs are used or sold. If you are thinking of starting – don't. You have got to be strong. When people pass you a joint or a pill or whatever, they are in fact saying, 'Let me spoil your life.' (Elizabeth, 22 cocaine user)

Designer drugs – a deadly game of chance

Seizures of ecstasy and reports of death and illness associated with the so-called 'dance drug' are escalating at a dramatic rate, police and doctors say.

Five people have died and at least 10 other people have been made seriously ill as a result of using 'ecstasy', mainly at 'rave' parties or nightclubs. Although the numbers are small in proportion to the estimated half a million users of ecstasy, its spiralling use has led to warnings to young people that the drug can have unexpected effects.

Sometimes this is due to adulterations with substances like heroin, methadone, amphetamine and caffeine, but doctors say some individuals can suffer, either from accumulative use or from an allergy to the drug.

Dr John Henry, head of the poisons unit at Guy's Hospital in London, said there had been a 'dramatic increase' in cases of adverse reactions to ecstasy this year. 'We have gone from an average of between 15 and 17 reports a month between 1988 and 1990 to about 30 or 40 cases a month as this year [1991] has progressed.' He added: 'It's like Russian roulette. People do not know what they are taking.'

Dr Henry said the reactions were a type of 'severe heatstroke', mental effects such as paranoia and, in fatal cases, an allergic reaction which resulted in internal bleeding.

'It is a very, very unpredictable substance and we need to know more about it,' he said.

The reports reaching Guy's match up with largely anecdotal stories circulating among 'ravers' about illness – including bleeding, vomiting and muscle pains – associated with the drug.

The *Independent* (28/12/91)

IN GROUPS

Why do some people start taking drugs? List all the reasons you can think of.

How do young people obtain drugs? What is your attitude towards people who sell drugs to young people?

What is your attitude towards taking drugs? List all the actions you could take if you found out a friend was taking drugs. What action (if any) would you take?

Elizabeth says, 'You have to be strong' if you are offered drugs. What does she mean? Discuss ways of coping with a situation in which someone is pressurizing you to join in and try something that you don't want to try.

ROLE PLAY

Act out a situation in which a doctor explains to a teenager the risks involved in taking ecstasy.

'You must be joking, I'm not taking that!' Act out a scene in which a teenager refuses to be persuaded to take ecstasy, then discuss the assertiveness techniques that people can use to say no.

Ecstasy – the 'dance drug'.

Ecstasy – the facts

▶ Ecstasy was synthesized in 1898, first marketed in 1914 as an appetite suppressor, then dropped when its side-effects were noticed. It was rediscovered in the 1960s by hippies and eventually banned in 1977.

▶ It is said to produce feelings of euphoria and heightened sensuality. Ravers say that it makes them lose their inhibitions. They get a buzz and feel like dancing all night.

▶ Ecstasy is imported from undercover laboratories on the Continent and in 1992 was selling for between £15 and £25 a dose. It is swallowed either as a pill or a capsule.

▶ It is a class A drug so the penalties for ecstasy are the same as for heroin and cocaine.

WHY DO YOUNG PEOPLE COMMIT CRIMES?

One in three burglaries, thefts and criminal damage incidents are committed by people under the age of 17.

'It tends to be a phase that a lot of adolescents go through as they are growing up. It's their way of rebelling against their parents and asserting their individuality.'   (Home Office spokesperson)

Why do you do it?

Olivia Nicolson talked to six young offenders about why they committed their crimes. Here is the sort of conversation she had:

Steve: Are you going to say something made me go out thieving? There's no one but me to blame for it. I made the choice, didn't I?

Me: What if everyone made that choice? Took anything they fancied? What if you were running the country, what would you do with thieves?

Steve: I'd have a finger cut off every time they nicked something.

Me: That wouldn't do much good. Once you'd got only eight fingers, you might as well only have seven.

Steve: Well (he stops to think), there'd be quite a difference between two and one, you might stop there.

Me: I suppose that's an idea. What does anyone else think about that? Who'd stop thieving if you knew your fingers were going to be cut off?

Everyone except one: I certainly would.

The one: I think it's disgusting the way all you lot just go round and nick things, and then laugh about it afterwards. It's completely wrong, you're just not thinking about the people you're stealing from.

Pete: Oh, I'd never steal from someone unless I felt they could afford it. And I'd never dream of thieving from small shops. In a way, I think I'm quite a good thief: I usually steal when I want to give my mum or sister a present. Like last year, just before Christmas, I hid under a bed in Debenhams, then when everyone had gone off home, I found this sports bag and spent all night choosing my Christmas presents. It was the best Christmas ever.

The one: I wouldn't have been able to sleep a wink if I'd done that.

Pete: You can't talk. Look at you, you burned down a school.

The one: That was a crime of passion, wasn't it? My parents told me they were getting divorced and my girlfriend left me all in one week.

Pete: Well, I'd say you're more dangerous than I am.

The one: All I know is that I'm not going to be doing it again, and you are.

Me: Now, Pete, what I'd like to know is, why do you do it?

Pete: Well, I wouldn't do anything that I thought was really wrong. I once nicked a charity box and thought that was really wrong, and now I can't go by one without emptying my pockets into it. I feel like Robin Hood sometimes.

Steve: What I don't understand is why there aren't more people who do thieve – what do those sociologist people say about that? Why do people obey the rules?

John: Well, that's obvious, isn't it? They'd lose their job or something, or they might-'ve puffed themselves up so much that if they got caught they wouldn't be able to look their neighbour in the eye.

The Spectator (7/10/89)

IN GROUPS

Discuss what Steve, Pete and John said to Olivia Nicolson. What do you think of their views and attitudes?

The ages at which boys commit most offences are 15 and 18. Why do you think so many boys aged 15 to 18 get involved in crime? Why does criminal activity decline as boys become young men in their 20s?

Why do you think girls commit far fewer crimes than boys? Appoint someone in the group to act as spokesperson and share your views in a class discussion.

SHOPLIFTING

Each year shops lose £2 billion through theft. Just under a third of shoplifting offences in one recent year were committed by young people under 17.

'There's a peculiar double standard about theft,' says Lady Philips, chairperson of the Association for the Prevention of Theft in Shops. *'People are indignant if someone steals from their house, but they think shops can afford the loss.'*

Top London store Harrods loses about £4½ million a year from theft, but Lady Philips claims small retailers suffer even more.

Lady Philips doesn't like the term 'shoplifting'. *'We're talking about plain theft,'* she says.

Sarah's story

'I first started shoplifting when I was 14. I was out shopping with my mum when I saw a lipstick that I wanted. She wouldn't buy it for me so I slipped in into my pocket when she wasn't looking. It was as simple as that.

'When I realized how easy it was to steal things, I would take something every weekend – make-up, clothes, records. It just became a habit and I would end up stealing for the sake of it.'

(Sarah, aged 17)

Jenny's story

To the outsider, 18-year-old Jenny has a bright future and no cares in the world. Studying for a business management degree, she hopes to get a good job at the end of it.

What no one knows, not even her family, is that she was recently caught stealing a tie and make-up worth £34 from a Birmingham store. She was charged with theft and is awaiting her court case.

'I haven't been able to tell anyone at all about it because I feel so ashamed and embarrassed,' she says. 'I'd taken small things from other shops before, even though I knew it was wrong. In a way it had become an addiction. I wanted to stop but I couldn't.'

Jenny is horrified at the prospect of ending up with a criminal record but she's glad she was caught before her problem got out of hand.

'I know I deserve to be punished and in a way I'm grateful to have been caught. I'll never shoplift again. Being taken to the police station and treated like a criminal is something I'll never forget.'

Woman's Realm (27/8/91)

IN GROUPS

Discuss why Sarah started to shoplift. Do you think this is how most shoplifting starts or do people often start because a friend dares them or pressurizes them into starting?

What is your attitude to shoplifting? Is it 'plain theft' or is stealing from a shop different from stealing from someone's home?

Why do you think young people shoplift – greed? envy? boredom? to be one of the group? to show off? to get their own back on society because they have other problems? any other reasons?

'Modern shops make shoplifting easy.' What do you think shops and shopkeepers could do to cut down shoplifting?

What do you think shopkeepers should do if they catch a young person shoplifting? Should they always call the police and inform the person's parents? What factors should they take into consideration when deciding what to do? If you were a shopkeeper, how would you deal with a young person you caught shoplifting?

ROLE PLAY

With a partner, role play a scene in which a teenager like Jenny has to tell one of their parents that they have been caught shoplifting. Take it in turns to be the teenager and discuss what it felt like having to confess to your parents what you had done.

Act out a scene in which a group of teenagers, who are planning to go shoplifting, put pressure on someone who doesn't want to go shoplifting to go with them. Take it in turns to be the person who doesn't want to go and practise ways of saying no. How easy was it to resist the pressure of the group?

CAR CRIMES

Doreen Smith waved a cheery goodbye to her friends outside the bingo hall as she set off home. It was 27 December 1990, and it had been a really wonderful Christmas.

As she hurried along the lane, just yards from her home, the car hit her.

It careered along at top speed in reverse and slammed her against a wall. Fifty-five-year-old Doreen never stood a chance. Onlookers gasped in disbelief and screamed: 'You've hit someone! Stop!'

Before their horrified eyes, the teenage driver rammed the car into forward gear, screeched a few yards up an alley and then, unbelievably, reversed, out of control, and crashed into Doreen again.

She lay motionless on the ground, as a desperate looking youth lurched from the car and sprinted away up the alley. People rushed forward to help Doreen. Southwick in Sunderland is a small town and everyone had immediately recognized the 16-year-old lad. He'd appeared in court just a couple of weeks before for stealing a car, and had been given a year's probation. The police arrived at his home soon after the accident, and took him into custody.

Doreen's daughter, Christina Walton, 31, shakes her head sorrowfully and says: 'I just couldn't believe it was really happening to my mam. I felt numb and bitter.'

Doreen suffered serious injuries and was taken to Newcastle General Hospital and put on a ventilator. She lived for just two days.

Chat (2/11/91)

In the UK in 1991 the number of recorded criminal offences was over 5 million – one crime every six seconds. One third of all new crimes were car crimes.

In 1991 nearly 500,000 cars were stolen. Most known car crime offenders were teenage boys – 34 per cent aged 15 to 16 and 39 per cent aged 17 to 20.

Cars stolen by joyriders are 200 times more likely to be involved in accidents. During 1990 and 1991, several people were killed in accidents caused by thieves. Some of those who died were young joyriders, others were innocent victims of the young drivers' recklessness.

As a result of these deaths and the car-related disturbances that occurred in Oxford and Newcastle in August and September 1991, the government introduced tougher laws. For the offence of Aggravated Vehicle Taking an offender can be sent to prison for up to 5 years, given an unlimited fine and banned from driving for life.

Why do joyriders steal other people's cars?
A sample survey of 14-year-old students gave the following anonymous answers:

- to impress friends **40%**
- to show off **30%**
- out of boredom **10%**
- to annoy car owners **4%**
- other reasons **16%**

Sean's Story

'I was 12 when I started. I just did it to be like everybody else in the gang. Eventually I got heavier into it and started stealing cars for burglary and that. I'm trying to stop it now but it's very hard because my mates all do it. Round here, there's plenty to do during the day, but not at nights. . . .

'It's hard to turn away from your mates, to say, like 'I don't want anything more to do with this.' If you did that you'd be more or less on your own. And you get girls, they get into the cars with you. So it sort of puts you up the ladder a bit within a group. . . .

'It's like a drug, adrenalin flowing, you get attached to that feeling. The younger ones just like it, then when you get older you can get money. Everybody knows you're a joyrider, so somebody will come up and say, 'Can you get me bits for my motor?' And you say, 'OK I'll get you four wheels for £100, a radio for £20 and seats are about £80.' That's a lot of money round here.'

The Independent (13/9/91)

The Ilderton Motor Project

Down at the Ilderton Motor Project, they don't believe prison is the answer to joyriding. Here, young lads who steal because they are addicted to the knife-edge thrills of racing at speed learn to redirect their desires towards a legal racetrack.

They learn to convert vehicles for banger racing and have to work for several weeks on a car before they get the chance to actually race. If they reoffend, or miss compulsory sessions, they are penalized by being moved to the bottom of the race rota.

Twenty-three-year-old Craig Cook has been coming to the project for nearly three years. 'When I was younger I was in prison a few times,' he says. 'I'd been sent on all sorts of projects, but none of them helped until I came here. This place really makes you think and see why it's wrong.'

Craig was banned from driving before he was even old enough to have a licence.

'I'm not proud of my experiences,' he says, 'but now I come down here to tell the boys what it's really like in prison and it puts them off.'

Every Wednesday, all the members of the project meet to discuss auto crime. They are encouraged to own up if they have reoffended or broken the rules. Then the members themselves decide on a penalty.

Project worker Trevor Hutchinson, explains: 'These young boys are blinded by wanting to drive. It's like a drug for them, they live for cars, and they just don't realize how serious a prison sentence is.

'As a member of staff it's very rewarding. You see them come here all geared up about driving – then, after a while, they start to regard the project as their own and to make their own decisions.

'Lots of the boys here have been through the whole criminal justice system and it hasn't helped them.'

Adapted from Chat (2/11/91)

The wreckage of a stolen car in which three teenage joyriders died after they crashed head-on with a police van.

You find out that your brother or sister has been joyriding. What do you say to them to try to persuade them not to go joyriding again?

'Are you coming or not?' Act out a scene in which a young person retains their self-esteem by refusing to go joyriding, in spite of being put under pressure to do so by their friends.

FOR YOUR FILE

Write a story about a teenager who has had a friend or relative killed in an accident caused by a joyrider.

IN GROUPS

How would you feel if it had been your mother or grandmother who had been knocked down and killed in the way Doreen Smith was?

What is your opinion of someone who goes joyriding? Do you admire them or do you think that they are behaving thoughtlessly and immaturely?

'A person who refuses to be pressurized into going joyriding is a stronger character and able to respect themselves more than a person who gives in to pressure and goes joyriding because they are afraid of being rejected by the group.' Do you agree?

What do you learn from Sean's story about why people go joyriding? Study the results of the sample survey. What do you think are the main reasons why people go joyriding?

What punishments do you think joyriders should be given? Do you think there should be more projects like the Ilderton Motor Project?

IN PAIRS

How serious is car crime?

A recent survey asked 150 teenagers to say which of five crimes they thought was the most serious. The result was:

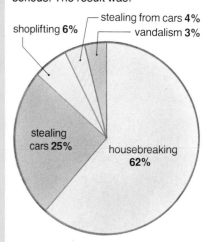

- stealing from cars **4%**
- shoplifting **6%**
- vandalism **3%**
- stealing cars **25%**
- housebreaking **62%**

List all the different crimes you can think of, then rank them in order of seriousness, starting with the most serious. When you have finished, form groups and compare your views.

WHAT'S YOUR VERDICT?

Criminal offences are divided into two types – summary offences and indictable offences.

A summary offence is an offence which can be tried in a Magistrates' Court. Examples of summary offences are: vandalism, being drunk and disorderly and most motoring offences.

Indictable offences are more serious offences, many of which carry penalties of several years' imprisonment. Indictable offences are usually tried before a judge and jury in a Crown Court.

Young people under 17 who are charged with a criminal offence are usually dealt with by magistrates in a Juvenile Court.

Types of sentence

When a person has been found guilty in a Magistrates' Court, the magistrates decide on the sentence. Often, they will ask for a social inquiry report. In deciding the sentence they take into account how serious the crime was, whether the person has been convicted before, why they acted as they did and what the probation officer suggests is an appropriate sentence.

Here are some of the main sentences that magistrates can give, arranged in approximate order of severity:

Absolute discharge   Even though the person has been found guilty, there is no penalty, usually because the offence was a minor one or the magistrates felt that it was committed due to circumstances outside the person's control. In Scotland, it is called an 'admonition'.

Conditional discharge   No punishment is given, on condition that the person does not get into further trouble with the law for a specified period, usually a year. If a further offence is committed during that time, they can then be punished for both offences.

Binding over   The person agrees to be 'bound over' to keep the peace (be of good behaviour) for a certain period of time. If they fail to do so, then the court will require a payment to be made.

Fine   The amount of the fine depends on the seriousness of the offence and the person's past behaviour. The law states the largest amount that you can be fined for a particular offence. The court has to take into account a person's ability to pay and time can be allowed for the fine to be paid at so much per week.

Community service   The person can be ordered to do between 40 and 240 hours of unpaid work that is of some value to the community.

Probation   The person has to report regularly to a probation officer, who supervises their behaviour and tries to help them to keep out of trouble. A probation order usually lasts for between one and three years.

Supervision order   Young offenders can be placed under a supervision order for up to three years. Often the court makes other requirements, the most common of which is a course of intermediate treatment (IT). This takes many forms but can involve attendance at a centre five days a week or once a week at the supervisor's office.

Outside: lawyers, space, grass.
Inside: warders, bars, cells.

Compensation order The court can order the person to pay compensation to the victim in a case, up to a maximum of £2,000.

Custodial sentence The person (if they are over the age of 21) is sent to prison. The law states the maximum prison sentence that can be given for each particular offence. The court can also give a suspended prison sentence. This means that the person does not go immediately to prison, but they can be sent there if they commit a further offence.

Boys aged 14 and over and girls aged 15 and over can be sentenced to detention in a youth offender institution. The minimum sentence is three weeks for boys and over four months for girls up to a maximum of 12 months.

Commitment to Crown Court for sentence If the magistrates think the person should get a longer custodial sentence than they have the power to impose, they can commit the offender to the Crown Court for sentence.

IN PAIRS

Study the list of offences (below). Decide what sentences you would give in each case to two teenagers found guilty of the offence: Gary, aged 17 with two previous convictions and Trevor, aged 14 with no previous convictions.

1 Theft of goods worth £60 from a supermarket.

2 Causing criminal damage of £1,000 on a building site.

3 Being in possession of cannabis – Gary 2 ounces, Trevor an eighth of an ounce.

4 Breaking into a house and stealing a video-recorder and some tapes.

5 Assaulting a woman aged 65, knocking her to the ground and stealing her handbag.

6 Being drunk and disorderly and causing a disturbance.

7 Taking a vehicle, which Gary drove, crashing into a lamppost and causing £4,500 damage.

8 Stealing a stereo, speakers and tapes from a car.

When you have finished, compare your decisions in either a group or class discussion.

IN GROUPS

Is prison the right place for criminals? Many people argue that putting offenders in custody is more likely to make them hardened criminals than to reform them. Discuss alternative ways of punishing offenders. In your opinion, what types of sentences are most likely to stop people re-offending?

You are a government committee which has to decide how to spend £10 million on a scheme for the treatment of young offenders. You can spend it either on increasing the number of custodial places or on an alternative scheme that the committee suggests. How would you spend the money?

FOR YOUR FILE

Write an article on teenage crime, saying why you think so many teenagers get involved in crime and how you think young offenders should be dealt with. Should there be tougher sentences? What types of sentence do you think are likely to deter young people from offending again and make them change their behaviour?

A CHOICE OF FUTURES

During the 1990s the world's population is likely to grow from 5.3 billion to 6.3 billion. United Nations figures suggest that the world's population will finally stabilize towards the end of the 21st century at about 11.6 billion. But unless there is progress in reducing birth rates, then the number could rise to 14 billion.

The growth in the world's population puts an ever-increasing strain on the world's natural resources and threatens the environment. According to Dr Nafis Sadik, Executive Director of the United Nations Population Fund, the situation is critical. 'The next ten years will decide the shape of the 21st century. They may decide the future of the earth as a habitation for humans.' *(The State of World Population 1990)*

Most of the 1 billion (one thousand million) extra people who will be added to the world's population this decade will live in the developing world. Slower population growth in developing countries and increasing economic growth without irreversible damage to the environment will depend on investment in women. This includes health care and family planning, education, granting women equal access to land, to credit and to rewarding employment, as well as establishing their personal and political rights.

WHAT CHANGES BIRTH RATES?

- Availability of family planning information and services
- Better health and fewer child deaths
- Improved status of women
- Later marriages
- Education and literacy
- More employment opportunities
- More equal income distribution and rising living standards

Adapted from a *Population Concern* leaflet

Choice and not chance

Population groups regard family planning in developing countries as essential to encouraging smaller families.

In China couples are encouraged to have only one child. The poster, above, is part of this campaign.

In the 20th century some countries have tried to stem the rapid growth in their populations. China, which is the most highly populated country in the world, with more than one billion people, has a 'one child' policy, under which women with only one child are awarded extra state benefits.

In the early 1970s in India, the government of Indira Gandhi set up several camps where men could be sterilized. Despite the offer of incentives, the response seems to have been unsatisfactory, because some men were reportedly rounded up and forcibly sterilized.

Today, however, most governments recognize that forcible methods of population control are undesirable. Instead, demographers (who analyse population changes) now concentrate on tackling factors which they believe lead to rapid population growth: poverty, the low status of women, high rates of child mortality, religion and the lack of family planning. Poverty is thought to act as an incentive to population growth because in poor families children act both as a source of labour and provide someone to look-after them in their old age. The more children the parents have, the more they consider that they have security. Economic progress to reduce proverty is therefore seen as one way of encouraging smaller family size.

However, the United Nations stresses that economic progress is a long-term strategy. Birth rates can be reduced even without improving standards of living. One approach is to provide more educational services, particularly for women. According to Marie Stopes International, the family-planning organization, women who are educated are more aware of the options open to them and more likely to practise birth control: they tend to have between one and three fewer children than those who are uneducated.

However, some couples do not practise birth control because their religious beliefs forbid them to do so. The Catholic Church, for example, is opposed to any artificial methods of contraception.

The UN suggests that another solution is to reduce the level of deaths among children through greater health care. 'Many parents compensate for the anticipated loss of children by giving birth to more than they actually want,' it says.

But most population groups now agree that the most effective way of stemming the growth in population is by extending family-planning services. The World Fertility Survey, carried out in 41 developing countries in 1985, concluded that there were at least 300 million couples who wanted to stop, or at least, delay having children but had no access to contraceptives.

COUNTRY A

CURRENT POPULATION: 20M

There is a poorly developed health system here, so the death rate is very high. But as family planning is not widely used, the birth rate is very high too. The overall population growth rate is four per cent per year – enough to double the population every 17 years.

The infant mortality rate is high too – around 70 per thousand live births – so any child born here will have a dangerous start to life.

DEATH RATE

10.5 per thousand

BIRTH RATE

50.9 per thousand

The government will struggle to pay for a minimum education for the increasing numbers of school-age youngsters. And it will not be able to improve educational standards. When a child grows to adolescence and is looking for a job, she or he will face fierce competition.

The labour force in the countryside will triple by 2025, so the amount of land per worker will decline, reducing food availability and standards of nutrition.

The population of Country A does eventually stabilize, but not until it has reached 120 million.

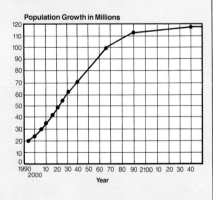

Population growth.

COUNTRY B

CURRENT POPULATION: 20M

With better health care facilities, infant mortality rates here are less than half those in Country A. And since all the population has access to family planning services, parents are in a position to choose to have smaller families.

The greater interval between births also increases the survival chances for both mother and child. Infant mortality is only around 33 per thousand live births.

DEATH RATE

6.3 per thousand

BIRTH RATE

22.5 per thousand

Standards of education are rising in Country B: with school numbers going up only slowly, more resources can be devoted to each child. Investment in agriculture will enable food production to rise. And with fewer farm workers needed, less than 50 per cent of the population will be engaged in agriculture.

The adolescent growing up in Country B is more likely to find a job in the city in industry or in the modern service sector.

Country B's population is going to stabilize at a much lower level than Country A's – 35 million – and much sooner.

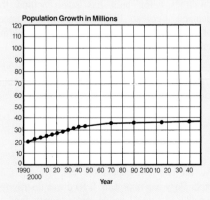

Population growth.

Adapted from a *Population Concern* leaflet .

IN GROUPS

The chart, 'What changes Birth Rates?' shows different ways that high birth rates can be reduced. Talk about each change in turn and say why it helps to reduce birth rates.

'Governments should offer incentives to encourage people to have no more than one child.'

'If voluntary methods don't work, then governments should force people to have small families.'

'It's a basic human right to have as many children as you want.'

Discuss these views.

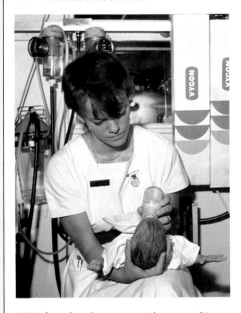

IN PAIRS

Imagine that you are the committee members of a charity called *Population Alert*. Your charity has raised £10 million to give to the world's poorest countries to help them to try to reduce their birth rates. Suggest some projects that you will use the money to support.

ROLE PLAY

The State of World Population Report, 1990 looked at the prospects for two hypothetical countries – A and B. Both have current populations of about 20 million but face very different patterns of population growth. Study the information about the two countries. Talk about the different types of future that children born in these two countries would be likely to face. List the reasons why Country A's population would probably grow so much greater and take so much longer to stabilize than Country B's population.

Population growth is a key factor in the two processes which currently pose the greatest threat to the environment: the degradation of soils and forests, and global warming.

THE THREAT TO THE ENVIRONMENT

Soil degradation and deforestation

Soil erosion is now a severe problem in the world. It is estimated that 6 to 7 million hectares of agricultural land are made unproductive each year because of erosion. The actual cause of most land degradation is loss of vegetation, but the underlying cause is people.

Forests and woodlands are cleared for farming and fuelwood. Where there is no more new land and farmers cannot afford fertilizer, the land they are already on becomes over used. The soil becomes less fertile and the vegetation becomes weak. In the tropics, land that has been cleared by burning, and planted with crops often loses its fertility in just a few years. Slowing population growth will slow down further degradation.

tremendous problems in these countries – many of which are already struggling.

Theoretically, it should be possible to grow enough food for everybody – but at what expense? For a start, every square metre of possible land would have to be used to produce a barely sufficient, mainly vegetarian diet, using large amounts of fertilizer and pesticides. As most of the potential land for this lies in the tropics, massive migrations of people would be needed to provide the necessary labour force and staggering amounts of the rainforests would have to be cleared.

This is obviously completely undesirable and unrealistic. We can in theory feed a growing population, but only with massive financial support to less developed countries, by huge social dislocation and by damaging the environment in a way which will have catastrophic consequences.

Global warming

The continuing build-up of greenhouse gases is altering the composition and behaviour of the atmosphere.

The major responsibility for the production of these gases lies with the industrialized countries. People living in the developed world each add on average around 3.2 tonnes of carbon into the atmosphere each year. This is four times the amount added by the average person in a developing country. This shows the disproportionate impact population growth in industrialized countries has. In fact, the additional 1.74 million Americans each year may well do as much damage to the environment as the 85 million added to the Third World.

But as the population of developing countries increases, so will their contribution to pollution. By 2025 developing countries will be emitting 16.6 billion tonnes of carbon dioxide annually – three times their present level. The number of cars in the world is set to grow from 400 million to 700 million by the year 2000. Much of that growth is expected to occur in the developing world, which currently owns only 12 per cent of the world's cars.

Urbanization

In recent decades, populations in urban areas have grown even faster than overall population growth. Constant increases in urban populations have stretched services to the limit and the future prospects for many urban areas look quite bleak. The main problems are housing, sanitation and transport. The number of permanent dwellings being built has fallen behind the demand. Between 1970 and 1988 the number of households without adequate sanitation mushroomed from 98 million to 340 million.

Uncontrolled growth threatens to overwhelm transport, health and sanitation systems in many cities.

Food

As the world's population has grown, food technology has improved. If food was distributed equally, the world would have enough food to feed everybody. But because of unequal distribution, millions of people do not have enough to eat. Most of the additional 1 billion people will be born in the less developed world. This will create

Water

Water is a finite resource. There is a fixed amount circulating within the Earth's system and it is unevenly distributed. Many areas, including most of Africa, much of the Middle East and nearly all of Australia, have severe water deficits.

There are about 2 billion people in the world who live in areas suffering from chronic water shortages. In some countries, the situation is extremely grave. Egypt already uses 97 per cent of its available water resources, although it uses only 40 cubic metres per person per year, one fiftieth of the UK's usage. Yet the population of Egypt is set to grow from 54 million to 94 million by 2025.

Not only is water availability becoming more limited, but water quality is declining. The industrialized countries of Europe and North America have dumped billions of tonnes of pollutants into their rivers. Added to this is the fact that measures adopted to clean up the water only tend to tackle the result rather than the cause.

IN PAIRS

Study the information on these pages and script a short item for inclusion on television's 'Newsround' programme, explaining what you have learnt about how population growth threatens the environment.

ROLE PLAY

You have been asked to make suggestions for a charity that you think that the school should support next year. Prepare a proposal, in the form of an interview, in which you explain the reasons for supporting the charity called Population Concern.

WHAT IS POPULATION CONCERN?

POPULATION

CONCERN

It is an independent charity with the following aims:

- To raise awareness about the nature, size and complexity of world population, especially as it affects the social and economic development of humankind.

- To help establish a balance between the population of the world and its natural resources and environment by means which promote human welfare, personal freedom and the quality of life.

- To raise funds in the UK for population and development programmes around the world in order to provide the knowledge and means of planned parenthood as a basic human right.

FOR YOUR FILE

Write an article for a teenage magazine – Why *you* should be concerned about the population explosion.

CHOICES AT 16+

When you are 16, you can choose from these options:

- A general education course such as taking more GCSEs or doing A or AS levels.

- A pre-vocational course or work experience which may help you to decide what kind of job you are looking for.

- A vocational course which will train you for a particular type of work.

- A place on a youth training programme (see page 78)

- A full-time job.

To some extent, your choice will depend on what is available in your local area. If you want to do a general education course, you may have to decide whether to stay on at school or to transfer to either a college of further education or a tertiary college. Vocational courses, leading to BTEC (Business and Technical Education Council) qualifications and NVQs (National Vocational Qualifications) are mainly offered by colleges of further education.

STAYING ON?

'I messed about at school and didn't get good GCSE grades, so I decided to leave and look for a job. But there aren't any jobs at present, so I've applied for a place on a youth training programme. If I don't get one, I don't know what I'll do, because I'm told I'm not entitled to any benefits. It's dead boring being unemployed and having no money. I'm beginning to wish I'd worked harder or even gone to college, like some of my mates did.'

(Jordan)

'I decided to stay on even though my GCSE results weren't as good as I'd hoped. It was the right decision, because it gave me more confidence and enabled me to improve my qualifications and to develop my skills. I've done two blocks of work experience which have helped me to find out what I want to do and next year I'm planning to go to college to do a BTEC course.'

(Annia)

'I stayed on at school to do my A levels and it's worked out well for me. I feel happy in familiar surroundings with teachers who know me and I've been able to keep up my music. My friend left and is doing her A levels at college, because the school didn't offer the subjects she wanted. She likes it there. She says there's a more adult atmosphere and she likes mixing with people from all sorts of different backgrounds.'

(Teresa)

WHAT DO YOU WANT?

The choices you make when you reach 16 will depend largely on what you want out of life. The quiz is designed to start you thinking about what you want. Consider each statement in turn and write down either Agree/Disagree/Not sure. Then, join up with a partner and discuss your answers. What do you learn from your answers about what your priorities are?

1 I'd rather have a well-paid job that's not very interesting than a poorly-paid job that's interesting.

2 I'd prefer a job in which I'm told what to do rather than one in which I'd have to take the decisions.

3 I'd rather have a secure job that makes less money than risk taking a job with more money that might not last.

4 I'd prefer to do something that helps people rather than to be involved in making or selling things.

5 Developing a career is more important to me than finding the person I want to share my life with or having a family.

6 I want to get out and start earning money now rather than to spend time being a poor student getting more qualifications.

7 I don't want to get bogged down in a career until I've had a chance to travel and see the world.

8 It's more important to me to do something that's meaningful and worthwhile than to make money.

9 I want to get enough skills and qualifications to make sure that I'll never be unemployed.

ROLE PLAY

What options are open to young people in your area at 16+? Study any booklets on your choices at 16+ that are produced by your local careers service or by the Training and Enterprise Council. Then, in pairs, role play a scene in which an expert advises a 16-year-old about the options open to them, and tells them where they can look for further information about courses, jobs and training opportunities in the local area.

IN PAIRS

What do you think are the advantages and disadvantages of staying on at school? In pairs, make a list of all the points that you think that a person should consider before deciding whether or not to leave school. You could arrange your list in two columns – For staying on/Against staying on. Then, join up with another pair and compare your lists.

WHAT IS YOUTH TRAINING?

Youth Training is a training programme which is designed to provide job training for young people. All young people who are not in full-time education at 16 or 17 are eligible for youth training.

WHAT ARE THE TRAINING PROGRAMMES LIKE?

The Training programmes vary according to the job. Within YT you can train for all kinds of jobs. The programmes are very practical and are designed to equip you with the skills you need in order to be able to do the job for which you are being trained. Most of the training is done at your place of work or the local College of Further Education.

At the start of your training programme, you will enter into a training agreement which sets out the training you will receive.

HOW LONG WILL THE TRAINING LAST?

Your training lasts as long as it takes for you to acquire the skills you need. That could be six months or less. The maximum length of time is usually two years.

CAN I BE EMPLOYED AND ON YT?

Many employers use YT as the first part of an apprenticeship, so you can be employed and on YT. Sometimes, an employer will take you on as a trainee and convert you to an employee during the course of your training when a vacancy arises.

WILL I GET PAID?

All trainees are paid a weekly training allowance. In some cases you may also get assistance with travelling expenses.

WHO DOES THE TRAINING?

The scheme is organized by the local Training and Enterprise Council. The training is given by lots of different organizations, including companies, Colleges of Further Education and special industrial training groups.

HOW WILL I KNOW HOW I'M GETTING ON?

A record of your progress and achievements is kept and you will be visited regularly by a supervisor in order to check-up on how you are getting on and to help you to sort out any problems.

WHAT QUALIFICATIONS WILL I GET?

All trainees have the opportunity to achieve NVQs – National Vocational Qualifications – at level 2 or above, or other accepted vocational qualifications. Each NVQ covers a particular area of work. If you have an NVQ, it shows that you have the skills to do a certain job to a nationally recognized industry standard. If you do well on your training programme, you can then go on to higher education.

HOW CAN I FIND OUT MORE ABOUT YOUTH TRAINING?

You can find out about Youth Training opportunities in your area from your careers teacher or local careers office.

ROLE PLAY

Study the information on this page and note down any important points that are made. Then, in pairs, act out a scene in which two young people, who are planning to leave school at 16, discuss youth training and what it has to offer them. Refer to your notes if necessary.

When you have finished, join up with another pair and discuss what you have learnt about youth training, and whether you would consider joining a training programme.

FOR YOUR FILE

Write a letter to a friend aged 16 who is thinking of applying for a youth training placement, telling them what you think the advantages of youth training are.

REVIEWING YOUR PROGRESS

The aims of this activity are:

- to give you the opportunity to review your progress in your courses.
- to discuss your achievements with your tutor.
- to produce a written record of your achievements.
- to plan ahead and set yourself targets for the future.

STAGE 1 SUBJECT REPORTS

Write a report on your progress in each of the subjects you are taking. Think of the skills and abilities that the course is designed to develop. Comment on your progress in each particular skill.

Compare what you write with any reports that your subject teacher has written about you. Discuss these reports, and your views on your progress, with each of your subject teachers.

STAGE 2 A DISCUSSION WITH YOUR TUTOR

Prepare for the discussion by listing everything that you have achieved during the year – both inside and outside the classroom. Then, discuss your views of your progress in your schoolwork and your other achievements with your tutor. What has gone well? Not so well? What are your strengths? Your weaknesses?

STAGE 3 A WRITTEN STATEMENT

After your discussion with your tutor, use a word processor to draft a statement that outlines your progress and achievements during the year. Show the statement to your tutor and discuss it. Agree any changes and additions to your statement. Then print out a final copy and put it in your file.

STAGE 4 SETTING TARGETS

Think carefully about what you need to do to make next year a successful one for you. Make a list of targets, starting with the most important one. It needn't be long. In fact, it's better to make a short, realistic list that you can keep to. Put your list of targets in your file, as a reminder of what you plan to do.

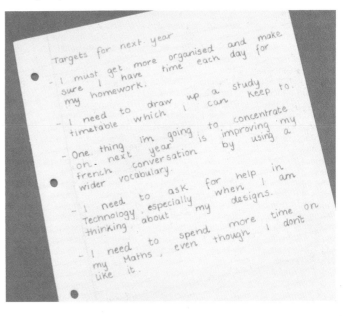

Acknowledgements

The following publishers, authors and agents are thanked for permission to reproduce extracts and copyright material:

The text on the Sex Discrimination Acts is adapted from a pamphlet *Equal Opportunities: A Short Guide To The Sex Discrimination Acts*, the Equal Opportunities Commission (page 6); the statistics about 'High-paid' and 'Low-paid' jobs are from the leaflet *Women at Work*, the Equal Opportunities Commission; 'How women lag behind' is an extract from the article *Europe Leads The Way On Women's Pay, Today* newspaper, 25 September 1992 (page 7); *I Got Stuck On A Junior Level* by Madeleine Bunting, The *Guardian*, 29 October 1991 (page 8); 'Feminism and equality' is adapted from the article *Loose Talk: What You Really Think About Feminism, Company* magazine (page 9); details of survey about sexual harassment are adapted from the article *Sex Harassment: Facts Of Life At Work* by Caroline Lees and Richard Palmer, © *Sunday Times*, 20 October 1991; *Use Your Common Sense, Men Told* by Tracey Harrison, *Daily Mail*, 1 February 1991 (page 10); quotations about pornography adapted from the article *The Glamour Game?*, *Mizz*, Issue 143 (page 11); the text on 'The Supply of Goods and Services Act, 1982' adapted from *Teacher's Fact-Sheet No. 5*, The Office of Fair Trading; 'Letters about unsatisfactory service from an article in *Square Deal* magazine, The Office of Fair Trading (page 14); in the section 'Mail order', the 'Golden rules' and the information on 'Buying books and tapes', 'Buying from a newspaper or magazine advert' and 'Buying from a catalogue' are all adapted from the leaflet *Buying By Post*, The Office of Fair Trading (page 15); the explanations 'What is Pre-Menstrual Syndrome?' and 'What causes PMS?' are adapted from the article *Pre-Menstrual Syndrome – Don't Suffer In Silence* by Annabel Goldstaub, *Just Seventeen*, 29 July 1987; 'Jenny's story' adapted from the article *PMS Made My Life Hell*, *Mizz*, Issue 177 (page 19); quotation by ex-acne sufferer from the article *Acne – The Causes And The Cures* by Fiona Gibson, *Just Seventeen*, 19 February 1986 (page 18); 'Tattoos' text adapted from an article by Robert Leedham, The *Guardian*, 14 January 1992 (page 19); 'What causes urbanization in the Third World?' adapted from pages 19/20 of *City Lights: Fatal Attractions? An Urbanization Education Pack of Student Resources* by Aileen Macenzie, WWF United Kingdom Education Department (page 20); 'Urban life or rural life – which would you choose?' adapted from pages 30/32 of *City Lights: Fatal Attractions?*, WWF (page 21); 'Inner city decay and urban sprawl' adapted from pages 4/5 of *The Urban Environment* by Kenneth Button, British Gas Publications (page 22); 'What is prejudice?', 'Racism' and 'Racial prejudice + power = racism' adapted from *Racism! What's It Got To Do With Me?*, British Youth Council (page 24); *Racism's Smiling Face Unmasked*, The *Independent*, 14 September 1990; extract 'Yet figures suggest . . .' from an article in The *Independent*, 11 October 1990; extract 'Employers are still . . .' from an article in the *Daily Mail*, 7 June 1991 (page 25); the three case studies from *Racism! What's It Got To Do With Me?*, British Youth Council (pages 26/27); survey and article *Young Can Overcome Prejudice Says Study* by Liz Lightfoot and John Quinn, The *Mail on Sunday*, 10 February 1991 (page 28); 'Cultural crossroads' by Apala Chowdhury, *Marxism Today*, October 1989; 'Tanuja's story' is an extract from the article *Culture Shock* by Brigit Grant, *Just Seventeen*, 4 November 1987; *Building My Own Island* by Hummarah Quddoos from *Knockout Poems*, Longman Publishers (page 29); extract on 'Attitudes to homosexuality' by Rosalyn Chissick *The Just Seventeen Advice Book*; 'Homosexuality and the law' adapted from the article *Out In Europe, Youth Clubs With The Edge*, Number 65, November 1991, Youth Clubs UK (page 30); 'Sally's story' and 'Mark's story' are extracts from the article *Hetero-Trans-Homo-Bi-A-Sexual* by Simon Geller, *Mizz* Issue 56; 'Myths about homosexuality' by Katherine King (page 31); 'How does worrying affect you?' adapted from the article *Don't Worry – By Happy, Jackie*, 23 'March 1991 (page 34); 'The 'hidden unemployed' by P Hammond (page 37); 'The economic cost' is an extract from *Unemployment* by Larry Elliott and Dan Atkinson, *EG*, 26 February 1991; quotation by Lord Scarman from *The Scarman Report: The Brixton Disorders* (page 38); quotations by Fatima, Abigail, Denise and Jackie are from *Girls Are Powerful* ed. Susan Hemmings, Sheba Feminist Publishers (page 39); 'What is the Greenhouse effect?' adapted from *The Environmental Science Reference Dictionary*, Harper Collins Publishers (page 40); the quotation in the section 'Combined heat and power' is from the article *Combined Heat And Power – The Solution?* by David Green, *Warmer Bulletin*, February 1992, The Warmer Campaign; the diagram 'An inefficient process' and the two facts quoted in the 'Conserving energy' section are adapted from the Friends of the Earth leaflet *Energy* (page 41); 'Disposing of nuclear waste' is an extract from the article *Power To The People* by Susan Richards *Geo* magazine, Series 13, Issue 2 (page 42); *For And Against Fission* by Richard Benson and Michael Brailsford, The *Indy*, 11 October 1990 (page 43); the diagram 'The nation's health' is adapted from page 3 of *EG*, 25 June 1991 (page 46); 'How do we compare?' text and table adapted from the article *Why Can't We Have Hospitals Like This?*, *Daily Mail*, 8 March 1991 (page 47); quotation by Afia, Erica, Mumtaz and Gillian are from *Speaking Out – Black Girls in Britain* ed. Audrey Ostler, published by Virago in their 'Upstarts' series (page 50); 'Friendship – the basic rules' from *A Means To a Friend* by Dr John Nicholson (page 51); 'The four types of love' adapted from *What Is Love?* by Julie Burniston, *The Mizz Book Of Love*; (page 52); *What Is Love?* by Julie Burniston, *The Mizz Book of Love*; 'The pressure to conform' is an extract from the article *You Can't Have a Bath During Your Period!*, *Just Seventeen*, 30 March 1988 (page 53); 'Breaking points' activity from page 25 of *Relationships* by Guy Dauncey, CRAC Learning Materials, Hobsons Publishing PLC; 'Donna's story' is an extract from the article *Yours Faithfully* by Jenny Tucker, *Just Seventeen*, 21 May 1986 (page 54); 'Heather's story' is an extract from the article *The Seven Deadly Sins of Love* by Andrew Wilson, *The Mizz Book Of Love*; 'What makes a relationship grow?' and the 'In Groups' discussion activity 'Dealing with disagreements' is adapted from page 25 of *Relationships* by Guy Dauncey, CRAC Learning Materials, Hobsons Publishing PLC (page 55); 'Why join a union?', the statement by Norman Willis and the section 'What will a union do for me?' from the TUC leaflet *Why Join A Union?* (page 57); 'Curbing the power of the unions' is an extract from *Unions* by Edward Pilkington, *EG*, 11 September 1990; 'A question of morality?' by Brigid McConville *The Role Of The Trade Unions* (page 58); 'Towards a striking new image' is an extract from *Unions* by Edward Pilkington, *EG*, 11 September 1990 (page 59); 'What do people think of unions?' is an extract from *Understanding Industry Now* by Rosemarie Stefanau, Heinemann Educational (page 61); *Young 'Drink To Reduce Pressure'*, The *Independent*, 1 September 1990; 'Some facts you should know' is an extract from *Sensible Drinking*, a pamphlet produced by Drink Wisely North-West, HEA (page 64); 'Designer drugs – a deadly game of chance' is an extract from the article *Ravers Play Russian Roulette With Ecstasy* by Terry Kirby, The *Independent*, 28 December 1991 (page 65); 'Why do you do it?' adapted from the article *Grandfather's Not To Blame* by Olivia Nicolson, The *Spectator*, 7 October 1989 (page 66); 'Sarah's story' adapted from the article *Criminals Learning Earlier*, The *Indy*, 11 January 1990; 'Jenny's story' adapted from *Shoplifting – A Crime Or A Cry For Help?* by Emma Lee-Potter, *Woman's Realm*, 27 August 1991; quotation by Lady Philips is an extract from an article on shoplifting by Alison Leah-Jones, *Woman*, 25 March 1991 (page 67); article about Doreen Smith from *The Road To Crime*, *Chat*, 2 December 1991; 'Sean's story' is an extract from the article *Belfast's Teenage Veterans* by David McKiltrick, The *Independent*, 13 September 1991 (page 68); 'The Ilderton Motor Project' text is an extract from the article *The Road To Crime*, *Chat*, 2 December 1991 (page 69); 'Choice and not chance' is an extract from the article *Population* by Edward Pilkington, *EG*, 10 September 1991; 'What changes birth rates?' is an extract from a *Population Concern* leaflet (page 72); information about 'Country A' and 'Country B' is from page 8, *Green Teacher*, Issue 21 (page 73); 'The threat to the environment' is adapted from pages 9/11 *Green Teacher*, Issue 21 (pages 74/75).

Photographs

The publishers would like to thank the following for permission to reproduce photographs (the page no. is followed, where necessary, by t-top, b-bottom, l-left, m-middle):

Associated Press Colour Library 42; Graham Bradbury 33, 35, 79r; Martin Bond/Environmental Picture Library 45t; Mills & Boons 52; CRE/HMSO 25; CSV/Sally Greenhill 70; Julian Calder/Tony Stone Associates 71l; Tony Craddock/Tony Stone Associates 40; Davis/Network 36t; Nigel Dickenson/Tony Stone Associates 74l; Thomas Braise/Tony Stone Associates 44r; Ben Edwards/Tony Stone Associates 20b; Franklin/Network 20; Goldwater/Network 73; Sally & Richard Greenhill 29; The *Guardian* 59; Crispin Hughes/Photofusion 50; Arnulf Husmo/Tony Stone Associates 59b; Hutchings/Network 22r; Hutchinson Library 72; Mick Hutson/Redferns 65; Martin Jenkinson 37, 56; Stephen Johnson/Tony Stone Associates 22l; Lewis/Network 18, 47; Steve Lillie 23, 39, 57, 66; Metropolitan Police Force 67; National Power Photo Library 44l; Adrian Neal/Tony Stone Associates 43; Lori Adamski Peek/Tony Stone Associates 63; Pemberton/Hutchinson Library 21r; Pam Isherwood/Format 30; Poulides/Thatcher/Tony Stone Associates 6; Press Association 68; Andy Sacks/Tony Stone Associates 36b; Steve Satuskeck/Tony Stone Associates 74r; Mike Shrimpton/Tony Stone Associates 71r; Anthea Sieveking/Collections 7, 8, 17, 27, 28, 38, 54, 76; Philip & Karen Smith/Tony Stone Associates 75; Sparham/Network 48; Tony Stone Associates 20t, 21l, 75t; Sturrock/Network 12, 58; Saffron Summerfield/Environmental Photo Library 32; David Sutherland/Tony Stone Associates 70; Sykes/Network 62; David Ximento Tejada/Tony Stone Associates 16; Chris Thompson/The Image Bank 11; Terry Vine/Tony Stone Associates 34; John Walmsley 27r, 78; Mo Wilson/Format 79l; Keith Wood/Tony Stone Associates 45b.